# Activate! 3

## enquiries into global citizenship

**Bhavina Algarra**

**General editor: Lee Jerome**

Published in 2002 by:
Nelson Thornes Ltd
Delta Place
27 Bath Road
CHELTENHAM
GL53 7TH
United Kingdom

02 03 04 05 06 / 10 9 8 7 6 5 4 3 2 1

A catalogue record for this book is available from the British Library

ISBN 0 7487 6021 0

Illustrations by Angela Lumley, Harry Venning and Peters & Zabransky
Page make-up by Clare Park

Printed and bound in China by Sun Fung

## Acknowledgements

The Institute for Citizenship and Nelson Thornes have developed the Activate! range of resources to provide a comprehensive response to the national curriculum for Citizenship at Key Stage 3. Activate! includes the following components:

Teacher's Starter File
Textbooks
Photocopiable resource pack
CD-Rom
On-line case studies

All have been developed in close consultation with teachers and the case studies and Starter File are the results of an extensive two-year pilot project.

The Institute for Citizenship is an independent charitable trust that works to promote informed active citizenship and greater participation in democracy and society. It was established in 1992 by the then Speaker of the House, the Rt Hon Bernard Weatherill, MP. The Institute develops and pilots innovative citizenship education resources, undertakes research and seeks to stimulate debate around citizenship issues. The work of the Institute for Citizenship is made possible through a wide range of local and national partnerships.

For further information visit www.citizen.org.uk

The Institute for Citizenship would like to thank Bhavini Algarra for additional material and would like to acknowledge the support of the following organisations:

The Bridge House Estates Trust Fund
The Equitable Charitable Trust
J P Morgan Fleming Educational Trust
Hackney Local Education Authority
Halton Borough Council

The authors and publishers wish to thank the following for permission to reproduce photographs and other copyright material in this book:
p 14-15 all cartoons reproduced with the kind permission of the Cartoonists and Writers Syndicate, 67 Riverside Drive, New York, 10024; p 26 Institute fel Tercar Mundo (1992), Third World Guide, Uruguay; p 27 Jubilee 2000 Coalition, p 36 (top left) reproduced by permission of Amnesty International Publications, Peter Benenson House, 1 Easton Street, London, WC1X 0DW, www.amnesty.org; p 37 Press Association; p 38 British Red Cross for the red cross emblem and use of the Society's name; pp 40-41 (all) International Committee of the Red Cross; p 42 Jubilee 2000 Coalition; p 43 Hulton Archive; p 45 International Committee of the Red Cross; pp 49, 52-54 Press Association; p 55 and 59 Jubilee 2000 Coalition

Every effort has been made to contact copyright holders. The publishers apologise to anyone whose rights have been inadvertently overlooked, and will be happy to rectify any errors or omissions.

# Contents

# Finding out – thinking about sources of information

**Effective action often requires us to become informed about a situation in order to understand why it is happening and what we could do to change it. Analysing the facts is often difficult because when we find information we have to think about where it came from, who said it and what were their reasons for putting that information together.**

Obvious examples appear in newspapers everyday, and many regular readers of newspapers understand the bias their paper has. Many individual journalists in newspapers also have their own well-known bias and some write for one political party or support a particular point of view. As readers get to know the bias of what they read, they often look out for the work of a particular author because they know they are likely to agree with that writer's point of view; at other times they will turn to pieces by different commentators because they want to think about alternatives or have their opinion challenged.

Bias is more difficult to assess when you do not know who the writer is or who they work for. Very often people will use the same facts to support different conclusions or select only those facts which support the message they want to get across. When carrying out your own research it is important to think about the following:

- What is presented as a *fact*? And can it be checked?
- In what ways is the information *biased*?
- What is the writer's *opinion*? And can you find alternatives?

Remember that being biased is not the same as straightforward lying, although you might still be misled.

A biased writer might use the following techniques to get his or her bias across:

- Add on their own opinion
- Quote only those people who share their opinion
- Use only certain facts to support their opinion and ignore others
- Interpret facts with their own comments.

### TASK

Authors use a range of techniques to get their point of view across. Look at the following examples and decide which techniques the writer is using.

(a) Wolverton United won a clear victory against their old rivals Totchester last night in a one-sided match in which Wolverton's skills shone out. Recovering quickly from a fluke goal against them in the first two minutes, Wolverton pinned down their opponents and mercilessly put a further two goals in the back of the Totchester net.

(b) Totchester were unlucky last night when their series of victories was interrupted for the first time in 10 matches. Starting the match as he had done twice this season, their star striker, Bazza, scored within the first two minutes. Injuring himself in the process, he was not taken off, all substitutes having been struck with a terrible virus the night before, and hobbled on through the match.

(c) Totchester started last night's game with a dazzling display of speed and wit by Bazza, driving home the first goal in seconds. Whilst Totchester literally limped on through injury and illness for the rest of the match they failed to achieve their early sparkle. Wolverton began to reclaim the initiative and maintained a 1–1 balance until the dying minutes of the game, when a decisive header from Rialdo gave Wolverton the match. In the end it was clear that Wolverton had played a blinder and thoroughly deserved to win – by far the better team on the day, and through history.

## TASK

Some information reflects the writer's opinions so clearly that it is possible to identify the author or organisation easily. Look at the three pieces of information in the panels below then decide which of the following organisations produced each one (answers on page 7):

(a) Oxfam

(b) Corpwatch: Holding Corporations Accountable

(c) World Trade Organisation

(1) *'The World Trade Organisation (WTO) is the only international organisation dealing with the global rules of trade between nations. Its main function is to ensure that trade flows as smoothly, predictably and freely as possible. The result is also a more prosperous, peaceful and accountable economic world. Decisions in the WTO are typically taken by consensus among all member countries and they are ratified by members' parliaments.'*

(2) *'Currently, developing countries account for three-quarters of the WTO membership, yet the WTO agenda is dominated by the interests of the major trading blocks and corporations.'*

(3) *'If anyone was in any doubt as to the true nature of the World Trade Organisation, its actions in the three years since it was created paint a depressingly clear picture. As feared, in every case brought before it to date, the WTO has ruled in favour of corporate interest, striking down national and sub-national legislation protecting the environment and public health at every turn.'*

### KEEPING TRACK

If you are researching a new topic, make sure you collect different opinions from a range of different organisations and authors. Organise them to see what facts they agree on and what the range of opinions is. This will help you to think about the topic from different points of view and understand it more thoroughly.

## TASK

Opinions can be clearly communicated in pictures and cartoons too. What do you think this cartoonist thinks of the WTO? Use the information on this page and on page 34 to make up your own cartoon about the WTO. You could choose to support it or attack it. Ask others in the class if they can identify your opinion from your image or cartoon.

# Justifying opinions

**Being biased is not necessarily a bad thing, it just means that we have to be aware of what the bias is, so we can understand the source of information properly. Lots of evidence that is biased is a deliberate argument, trying to convince the reader to agree with the author's point of view. In this case the bias will be easy to spot, but you then have to ask yourself how convincing is the argument? Has the author justified their opinion enough to convince you to agree with them?**

Look at the following example of an argument that might provide useful evidence in a project or piece of research. The researcher has written notes on the evidence in the table below.

## Coming to Africa's aid has been no help

**by Michael Dynes**

THREE hundred billion dollars of Western taxpayers' money has been sunk into sub-Saharan Africa in so-called development assistance over the past 50 years and there is virtually nothing to show for it.

Despite this tidal wave of aid, millions of Africans are poorer today than they were in the 1970s. Africa is now home to more poor countries than any other continent, with 34 of the world's 40 most impoverished nations.

Two conclusions present themselves, one blindingly obvious, the other bordering on heresy. Clearly, economic development has failed comprehensively in Africa. Everybody agrees on that. But whatever factor or combination of factors is needed to enable an economy to flourish on African soil, it is reasonably safe to assume that aid is not among them.

Aid has not only failed to stimulate growth; it has probably sabotaged any prospects the continent may have had for development.

Five decades of development assistance have left Africa with a crushing $350 billion debt, which takes two fifths of government revenues to service. Take away the immunisation programmes, and Africa or the West would be hard-pressed to explain where all the money went. In the Democratic Republic of Congo, to name but one, they are still paying off a $14 billion debt run up by the late President Mobutu, with no schools, hospitals or roads to justify it.

Over the past half century, most of the bright stars of Africa – Ghana, Kenya, Zambia, Nigeria, Uganda, Zimbabwe, and the Ivory Coast – have been snuffed out. After 50 years of failure, Western countries are suffering from what is politely known as 'donor fatigue'. Stripped of its politically correct vocabulary, the West thinks Africa is 'a basket case', a 'continental ghetto', a 'lost cause', and there is nothing anyone can do about it.

*The Times*, 23 November 2000

| Facts | Opinions | Comments |
|---|---|---|
| $300 billion aid to Africa in 50 years | Economic development has failed in Africa | Are there any examples of economically successful African countries? |
| Africa has 34 of 40 poorest countries in the world | Aid has made things worse | Research World Bank and/or non-governmental organisations (NGOs) to find successful examples |
| $350 billion debt (40% government revenue goes on repaying debt) | Much of aid money wasted | How much was wasted and how much used properly? |
| | The West thinks Africa is beyond help | What do Western governments actually say and do about Africa? |

# Levelling mountain of misery – Britain is winning the battle to alleviate developing countries' debt burden

by Gordon Brown and Clare Short

The lessons of recent years are that policies for debt relief, poverty relief and economic development must go hand in hand. Debt relief is both a moral and economic issue: money spent on servicing debt could be better spent on education and health. An overhang of debt, inherited from the past, should not prevent economic development in the future. Quite simply, the poorest countries cannot build for the new century on a mountain of unsustainable debt.

A third of the world's children go to bed hungry; 30,000 children die every day from preventable diseases; 1.3 billion people, two-thirds women, are in poverty. At the same time, they have to shoulder a multi-billion debt burden.

It is to move this previously immovable mountain of debt that Britain has made proposals now being examined by the international community.

In 1997, when we came to power, only one country had entered the highly indebted poor countries initiative. Now, as a result of world pressure and action, there are nine.

And, because debt reduction, poverty reduction and economic development must go together, we are determined to ensure that the billions saved from debt payments are put to work and invested in health, education and economic development of the countries concerned.

Now as never before, our generation has within its grasp the means to eliminate the injustice of abject poverty. Martin Luther King spoke of the inescapable network of mutuality – our common interests and shared responsibilities – that make a global economy into a single moral universe. He considered that an injustice anywhere is a threat to justice everywhere. As we leave the 20th century behind, let us leave behind this injustice, too.

*The Guardian*, 22 February 1999

## TASKS

1 Draw out a table like the one on the previous page and complete it for the article here.

2 Does having both articles help you to understand more about the issue?

3 What are the main differences between the opinions?

4 What does each article do well, to justify its position?

5 Do you think one of the arguments is more convincing than the other?

## KEEPING TRACK

When you are writing reports or planning for a debate, remember to think about the ways you build your argument. If it looks as if you are just putting your own ideas forward without evidence, people are more likely to dismiss what you say. If you can provide evidence to back up your opinion you can be much more convincing.

**Answers from page 5:** 1 – c; 2 – a; 3 – b

# Debates and debating

**Preparation is very important to a successful debate, but a debate should be more than just taking it in turns to read out speeches. You need to be able to respond to what other people say: thinking on your feet, questioning what others say and picking holes in their argument are important parts of exploring an issue through debate.**

There are many ways in which you can do this and you should think about the most appropriate method in each case.

**Debate Point**

**(1) Fault the logic**
Show that the conclusion does not follow from the evidence presented.

**(2) Question the evidence**
Argue that the evidence used is wrong or has missed out other important facts.

**(3) Admit the point**
Admit that the person has a good point but there is something else they have ignored. Simply provide an alternative set of facts and your own conclusion.

**(4) Appeal to authority**
Refer to someone else in the debate, especially well-respected people, who disagree with the speaker.

**(5) Lead the speaker**
Present facts from your own argument one by one to the speaker; as they accept each of your facts they will be drawn closer and closer to agreeing with you.

**(6) Challenge**
Ask the speaker to provide evidence for their view, and then evidence for their evidence – young children sometimes do this by asking 'Why?' to every explanation.

This may sound confusing but the example on the next page will help to make it clear.

Do you know every poor person in the world? How can you generalise about them?

Many people are poor because the countries they live in are poor. You cannot treat a country and a person in the same way because they are completely different.

Is it the case that poor people are lazy or have something wrong with them? It seems to me that many of the poorest people in the world work very hard just to enable themselves and their families to live. This probably involves more hard work than the rich actually do.

'People are poor because they do not want to work or are lazy or there is something wrong with them. It is no good blaming other people, they need to get off their own backsides and do something for themselves. The same goes for countries as for people, poor countries should look after themselves.'

Coal miners work very hard don't they? (YES)
But the coal mining industry in the UK is closing down isn't it? (YES)
And that means many miners lose their jobs? (YES)
And there are not many alternative jobs in the mining villages are there? (NO)
So would you say an unemployed miner looking for work is suddenly lazy? (NO)
But they are likely to be poor whilst they are unemployed aren't they? (YES) So that proves you were wrong.

You have certainly hit the nail on the head for a small minority of poor people. But you have to look at the actual circumstances of many poor people around the world to see that there are other more complicated reasons for poverty.

That is all very well but if you took a while to read some of the work of the economist Amartya Sen you would soon realise that all the facts point to a completely different conclusion.

## TASKS

1. Read the responses in the second spider diagram. Can you match them up to the numbered headings in the first one?
2. Working in pairs or small groups, choose a debate topic that you all know something about. Make a point each and try to come up with a response matching one or more of the headings in the first spider diagram.
3. Can you think of any other ways you could respond to an argument in a debate?
4. Have a classroom debate in two teams, for and against a motion. Each team could be awarded points for the quality of their responses. Keep a running total to see how well you do.

## KEEPING TRACK

You can plan your responses by thinking ahead and trying to predict the kinds of arguments your opponents are likely to use. You can then come up with arguments to defeat them or show their weaknesses. Remember to make notes and also further develop your own speeches for debates in the light of what people say in class. Write down what is said in the debate to remind you of all the arguments people put forward, and use other people's points of view to help develop your own opinions.

# Making a difference

**Knowing about a situation and being clear about your own opinions are the first steps to being able to get involved and help to change things for the better. The rest of this book is about global issues, and it often seems more difficult to influence decisions and events in other countries. But there are plenty of examples of how individuals in Britain can make a big impact on global issues.**

### Hackney Education Authority

Staff were concerned at the amount of waste which is being dumped in the earth and the long-term effects this will have on the environment. One of the first things they have done is to collect all the scrap paper in schools and make sure it is recycled. This adds up to tonnes each year which would otherwise have ended up in landfill sites.

### Red Noses

Many schools collect money during non-uniform days and other special events to pass on to Comic Relief. This money, over £20 million a year, is then spent all around the world, from local initiatives to farming projects in Africa.

### Dave the Builder

Dave uses lots of wood products in his job, ranging from floorboards to doors and even paintbrushes. He watched a TV documentary about the destruction of rainforests and decided he would buy products from companies that were trying to protect the environment. He searched the Internet to check out his local suppliers. Now he uses a store that says over 99% of all its timber products are from forests that are well-managed, and that have certificates from international organisations to prove this. This means Dave's work has less of a negative effect on the environment around the world.

### City Farm

Having read about global warming and pesticide pollution one group of parents and their children, in East London, are learning how to grow food organically. They will not use any chemical pesticides and they know that the food that they eat is clean and healthy. The parents and young people have also made good friends while doing the project, and have learned some useful skills.

### Fair Trade

Mary had finished a geography project on 'work' around the world and was shocked to discover how little of the money she paid for luxuries such as chocolate went to the farmers who grew the cocoa. She now buys fair-trade chocolate, which guarantees more money for the farmer.

### Heal The World

A group of students in a secondary school set up their own club with their geography teacher. One of their aims was to raise awareness about global issues among the other students and they planned campaigns around the school. Lots of their special events were tied into global events such as 'Women's Day' and they also tried to link school issues, such as equality, to issues around the world.

### European Issues

Students in Rushey Mead School made learning about European citizenship fun and interesting by linking it with the European Cup football competition. Teams researched their country and learned from each other as well as playing football. Once the competition was over, students knew a lot more about Europe and better understood their role in the EU.

### Amnesty International

Many schools have started Amnesty clubs. Amnesty monitors human-rights abuses around the world and campaigns for human rights to be respected. It achieves this by targeting a particular person in government and asking members to write to that individual, putting pressure on them to release prisoners of conscience. Often several thousand people will write to that one person.

### Voluntary Service Overseas (VSO)

Many young people and professionals volunteer with VSO every year. This organisation matches up the skills of its UK volunteers with communities abroad that need training. The volunteers can go and work in another country, and are paid enough to live according to local standards.

### Appeals

When an earthquake destroyed cities in northern India in 2000, many individuals and organisations held local events specifically to raise money for that one appeal. People also undertook sponsored activities and donated money which went straight to help with the rescue and aid teams.

## TASKS

1. Read through all the examples of action on these pages and list them under the following headings:
   (a) Think Globally, Act Locally
   (b) Consumer Power
   (c) Raise Awareness
   (d) Provide Direct Support
   (e) Take Direct Action
2. Which of the activities (a–e) in Task 1 have you been involved in? What did you do and how do you think it helped? (If you have not been involved in any of these activities yet, think of someone else you know who has and ask them the questions.)
3. Which type of action do you think is most useful?
4. Can you think of a group or organisation that is involved in each of these types of activities?
5. When is the next opportunity for you to get involved in one of these activities?

### KEEPING TRACK

Plan for some kind of action this year and build up to it. Find out who you have to contact and what you need to know before you get started. Think about the time frame and who else might be involved. Think also about the skills you will need to make your involvement successful.

# Our world, our rights?

**This section introduces you to the Universal Declaration of Human Rights (UDHR) and asks what rights are and whether they really exist for all people in all societies. There are no easy answers when thinking about human rights. It is up to you to make up your own mind on how important human rights are. How do we protect these human rights and how do we take responsibility for making sure our rights and the rights of others are respected?**

This is a shortened version of the Declaration. You can see the real thing at: www.un.org

**Article 1** Right to equality
**Article 2** Freedom from discrimination
**Article 3** Right to Life, Liberty, Personal Security
**Article 4** Freedom from slavery
**Article 5** Freedom from torture or degrading (meant to humiliate) treatment
**Article 6** Right to be recognised as a person by the law
**Article 7** Right to equality before the law
**Article 8** Right to a fair hearing if your rights are broken
**Article 9** Freedom from arrest with no reason and exile (being sent away)
**Article 10** Right to a fair public hearing if accused of something illegal
**Article 11** Right to be considered innocent until proven guilty
**Article 12** Freedom from interference with privacy, family, home and correspondence (e.g. letters)
**Article 13** Right to free movement in and out of the country
**Article 14** Right to asylum in other countries (safety) if being persecuted at home
**Article 15** Right to a nationality and the freedom to change it
**Article 16** Right to marriage and family
**Article 17** Right to own property
**Article 18** Freedom of belief and religion
**Article 19** Freedom of opinion and information
**Article 20** Right to meet peacefully with others and join groups
**Article 21** Right to participate in government by voting and standing for election
**Article 22** Right to social security
**Article 23** Right to work safely for equal pay and to join a trade union
**Article 24** Right to rest and leisure
**Article 25** Right to an adequate living standard
**Article 26** Right to an education
**Article 27** Right to participate in cultural activity, e.g. the arts
**Article 28** Right to have society run in a way which protects your rights
**Article 29** Everyone has duties but these should only help to achieve everyone's rights in society, they cannot harm rights
**Article 30** Everyone should be free from interference in their rights

## USEFUL WORDS

**Convention** – an international agreement

**Covenant** – a legal document

**UN Articles** – sections in a written document that refer to specific rights

**Treaties** – a formal agreement between two or more countries

**Aspire** – a strong desire to achieve something

**Boycott** – To refuse to buy a product as a protest

**Kurds** – An ethnic minority group in Iraq

**Sanctions** – A punishment for breaking international law

**Humanitarian relief** – Support provided for people's basic needs

## SKILLS FOCUS

- Thinking about rights and developing your own opinion about them
- Discussing topical issues

## Key points in the history of human rights

1948 Universal Declaration of Human Rights, part of the International Bill of Rights
1950 European **Convention** on Human Rights and Fundamental Freedoms
1951 Convention Relating to the Status of Refugees
1961 European Social Charter (under the Council of Europe)
1966 International **Covenant** on Economic, Social and Cultural Rights
International Covenant on Civil and Political Rights
International Convention on the Elimination of All Forms of Racial Discrimination
1969 American Convention on Human Rights (Latin America and the Caribbean)
1979 Convention on the Elimination of All Forms of Discrimination Against Women
1981 African Charter of Human and People's Rights
1985 Recommendation of the Committee of Ministers of the Council of Europe on 'Teaching Rights and Learning about Human Rights in Schools'
1989 Convention on the Rights of the Child
International Labour Office Convention on Indigenous and Tribal Peoples
1993 World Conference on Human Rights (Vienna Declaration and Plan of Action)
1994 UN General Assembly declares 'Decade for Human Rights Education'
1998 Human Rights Act (UK)

# Human rights – respected by everyone?

**The UDHR was followed by other UN Articles, treaties and conventions. All of them are designed to give basic rights to the individual. Many countries, once they have signed the treaties, do not implement them. But the treaties and conventions do stand for something: they lay down standards to which countries can aspire, and democracies across the world do their best to honour them.**

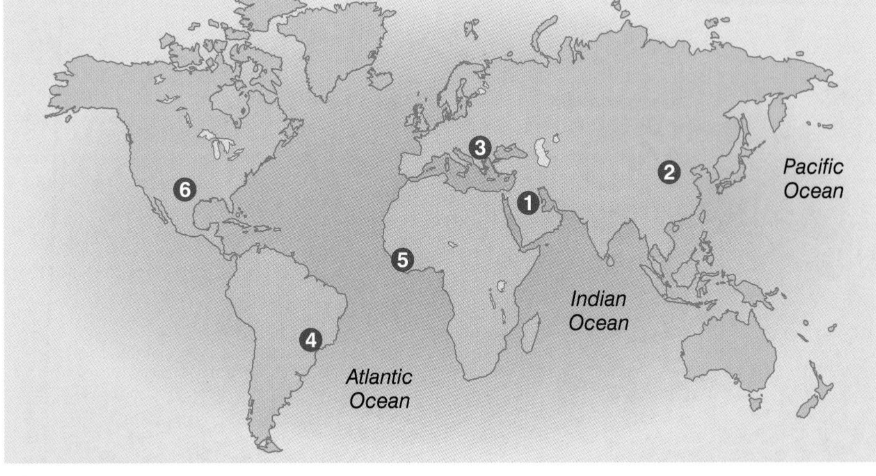


▲ Hot spots of human-rights abuse

### Saudi Arabia

This country is an oil-rich country in the Middle East. There is a government-enforced ban on all political parties and trade unions. People with different political or religious views from the government can be arrested and jailed for long periods of time without being charged or given a trial. Women are not allowed to vote or drive cars in this country. At least 103 executions took place in 1999.

### China

In 1999 the government restricted any form of peaceful demonstration. Thousands of people were detained for exercising their rights to freedom of expression or religion. Labour camps to 're-educate' these people were set up. Torture, including the use of electric shock, sleep and food deprivation, is widespread. According to Amnesty International, in 1999 at least 1,077 executions were carried out. Prisoners are frequently denied medical care and family visits.

### Yugoslavia

In the late 1990s there was a systematic programme to expel the non-Serbian civilian population from the Kosovo region. The police and soldiers killed thousands of ethnic Albanians, many of whom were raped and beaten, and their houses burnt. On several occasions the police used force to break up demonstrations during which hundreds of protesters were beaten.

### Brazil

This country is famous for its rainforest and carnivals. But it also has an appalling human-rights record. Torture is reported to be common in many police stations. Police and 'death squads' linked to the security forces continue to kill civilians, including children. Human-rights defenders have been threatened and attacked.

### Sierra Leone

Thousands of civilians, including the old, women and children, have been executed, mutilated, raped or abducted for no apparent reasons by both the rebel forces and the government forces. Over 5,000 children have been reported missing; many of them have been forced to become soldiers.

### USA

This country is one of the richest in the world. In 1999 more prisoners were executed than in any year since 1951, 98 in total. Police brutality, death in custody and ill-treatment of prisoners were reported. The number of women prisoners has tripled since 1989 and there have been reports that sick and pregnant prisoners have been restrained using force. Sexual abuse by male staff is also commonly reported.

Information and data from Amnesty International Report 2000

## TASKS

1 Using an atlas to help you, name the countries that are numbered on the map. Then copy the chart below and complete it using the information underneath the map.

2 The number of examples of human-rights abuses shown on the map is very small. Can you think of any other countries where human-rights abuses take place?

| Human-rights abuses | | | | |
|---|---|---|---|---|
| Where | When | By whom? | How? | Possible reasons |
| | | | | |

# And are we all treated equally...?

TURNER. Ireland

JAVAD. Iran

PETRICIC, Yugoslavia

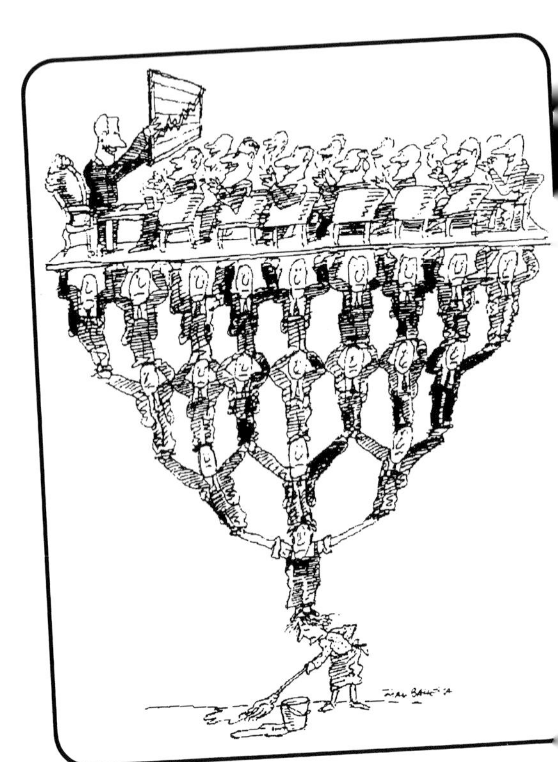

MOIR, Australia

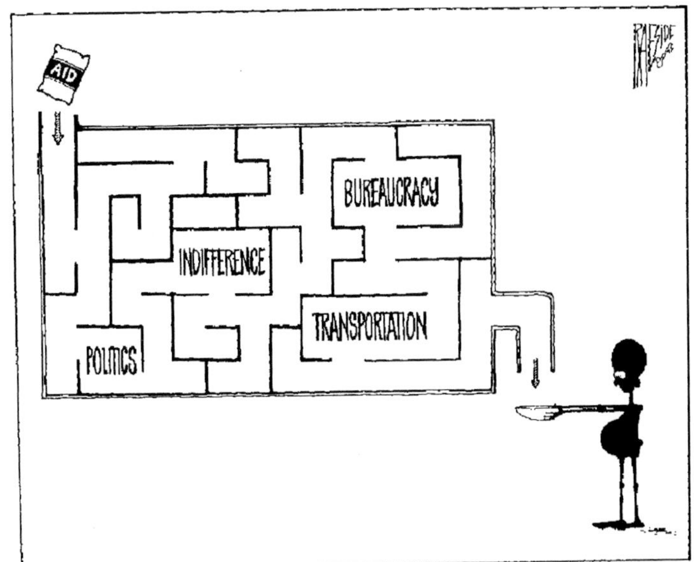


RAESIDE, Canada

KAL, USA

ARCADIO, Costa Rica

## TASKS

1. Think of a suitable heading for each of the cartoons, referring to human rights.
2. Make a list of the human-rights issues highlighted by these cartoons.
3. From your understanding of these cartoons, who is abusing whose rights?
4. Which of the cartoons do you think has the biggest impact? Give reasons for your choice.
5. Draw your own cartoon highlighting a human right.

# Iraq – paying the price; human rights or human wrongs?

### 1. Background: The West and Saddam Hussein

Saddam Hussein became President of Iraq in 1979. During the early 1980s Iraq was at war with its neighbour, Iran, and the West supported Iraq by providing it with money, weapons and information.

### 2. Key events in the Gulf War

**1990** **2 August**
Iraqi army invades Kuwait

**6 August**
UN declares a trade **boycott** against Iraq

**8 August**
USA starts sending troops to the area

**15 November**
UN Security Council gives the USA and its allies permission to use force against the Iraqi army

**1991** **17 January**
Fighting starts. The allies (the USA, UK and France) have 580,000 troops in the region (against 540,000 Iraqi soldiers)

**28 February**
Iraq withdraws from Kuwait and agrees to the UN Resolutions

The West continued to insist on two points:

- that UN Inspectors should be allowed to visit weapons sites to stop Iraq developing their weapons
- the West should maintain a 'no-fly' zone in which Iraqi planes were banned, to protect the **Kurds** who had been bombed.

### 3. UN Resolutions

UN Resolution 661 of 6 August 1990 is still in force (with some adaptations). It demanded that all countries should prevent:

- any imports from Iraq
- any activity to promote trade with Iraq
- any shipping of goods to Iraq EXCEPT food and medicine for **humanitarian relief**

and agreed that governments should not:

- make money available to Iraq.

UN Resolution 687 of 3 April 1991 demanded that Iraq allow the destruction of:

- all chemical and biological weapons
- all missiles with a range greater than 150km.

In 1996 the 'Oil for Food Programme' was introduced. This allowed Iraq to sell some of its oil and spend two-thirds of its income on food and medicine, with the rest being paid to Kuwait as compensation for the invasion.

In August 2000, the Iraqi government refused any more humanitarian aid saying 'Iraqis are not lazy people who ask for help'.

### 4. The US government's views of the sanctions against Iraq

'Saddam is diverting food to his favourites and storing supplies for the military.'

'This is not a UN problem, this is not a world community problem, this is an Iraqi government problem.'

(Both quotes by Thomas Pickering, Official of the US State Department)

### 5. The UK government's views of the sanctions against Iraq

'Despite the efforts of the UN the Iraqi government has yet to accept its responsibility for ordering enough medicines.'

'We must nail the absurd claim that sanctions are responsible for the suffering of the Iraqi people.'

(Both quotes by Robin Cook, Foreign Secretary)

'The people of Iraq have suffered too much.'

'Saddam manipulates the suffering of his people and uses it for propaganda. But we must do all we can to relieve the suffering.'

(Both quotes by Clare Short, Secretary of State for International Development)

### 6. Life in Iraq since the sanctions were imposed

- 4,000 children a month die
- Literacy rate has fallen
- Health service has declined
- Worsening water supply leads to more deaths through dysentery
- Increase in malnutrition
- Power cuts are more frequent
- Shortage of fuel supplies
- Inflation is very high
- General shortage of basic foods and medicine
- On-going problems with the export of oil because of limits imposed on equipment.

'I am resigning because the policy of economic sanctions is totally bankrupt. We are in the process of destroying an entire society. It is as simple and as terrifying as that.'

(Dennis Halliday, Coordinator of Humanitarian Relief to Iraq and Assistant Secretary General to the UN, March 2000)

### 7. Iraq's human-rights record

'Suspected political opponents, including possible prisoners of conscience, continue to be arrested. Scores of Kurdish families were forcibly expelled from their homes and members of targeted families detained. Torture and ill-treatment of prisoners and detainees is widely reported. According to reports, at least six people had their hands amputated as punishment. There was no further news on the fate of thousands of people who "disappeared" in previous years. Hundreds of people, including political prisoners, were reportedly executed; some without trial. Death sentences continued to be imposed, including for non-violent offences. Human-rights abuses were reported in areas under Kurdish control.'

(Adapted from Amnesty International's Annual Report, 1999)

### 8. Protestors against sanctions

Voices in the Wilderness is a group campaigning against 'the West's crippling economic sanctions against Iraq'. One of its members, a Mr Rolstone, called the UK policy 'a crime against humanity'.

Cambridge University students have set up an organisation called the 'Campaign Against Sanctions on Iraq' (CASI). They said: 'One only has to scratch away the shiny surface of the British government's rhetoric on Iraq to reveal an altogether different story, in which the civilian population of Iraq is paying a deadly price for its leader's crimes.'

## TASKS

Answer the following questions:

(a) What are the problems of the Iraqi people?

(b) Explain how each of the following has helped to cause or improve the situation:
- the UN
- the USA government
- the UK government
- Saddam Hussein.

(c) For each of the above, suggest how they could help to solve the problems of the Iraqi people.

(d) What would your advice be to the UK government about its dealings with Iraq?

# The world on our doorstep

## SKILLS FOCUS

- Discussing controversial issues and developing your own opinion

As travel becomes cheaper, it is easier for people to relocate from one country to another. People choose to work or study in new countries, move where the chances of a good life are better or sometimes have to run away from dangerous situations in their home countries. Many people also travel for sheer pleasure, wanting to see as much of the world as they can. All of this means that the communities in which we live are becoming **diverse**.

## Diversity in the UK

| Ethnicity | Number of people |
|---|---|
| White | 53,100,000 |
| Black Caribbean | 500,000 |
| Black African | 400,000 |
| Indian | 900,000 |
| Pakistani | 600,000 |
| Bangladeshi | 200,000 |
| Chinese | 200,000 |
| All other groups | 900,000 |
| Total | 56,800,000 |

| UK religions | Membership |
|---|---|
| Anglican | 27,000,000 |
| Roman Catholic | 9,000,000 |
| Muslim | 1,000,000 |
| Presbyterian | 800,000 |
| Methodist | 760,000 |
| Sikh | 400,000 |
| Hindu | 350,000 |
| Jewish | 300,000 |

The UK's foreign-born population pay 10 per cent more to the state than they get back in benefits and services – equivalent to £2.6 billion per year net. They push up the rate of economic growth and, for example, ensure we are treated when we are ill. Nearly 30 per cent of UK doctors and 13 per cent of nurses are non-UK born; half the extra **NHS** staff employed over the past decade qualified abroad.

*"150,000 non-EU, non-UK people are expected to arrive in 2001 with a view to long-term residence. Returning UK citizens form the biggest category of long-run settlers, mainly because from 1945 to the 1970s the* ***migrant*** *flow went heavily the other way."*

Extract from David Walker in *Guardian Society*, 29 January 2001

Nearly 4 million people (7.3 per cent of the total population) resident in Great Britain at the 1991 census had been born elsewhere in the world (including Ireland, north and south). The majority (61 per cent) were white.

### USEFUL WORDS

**Diverse** – mixed, varied

**NHS** – National Health Service

**Migrant** – someone who leaves one country for another

**Tolerance** – allowing people to be different without interfering with them

**Controversial** – something about which people do not agree and which they discuss at length

**Discriminate** – act unfairly against people on racial, religious, sex grounds, etc.

**Immigrants** – people who leave their country to come into yours

# London: Multilingual Capital of the World

By Andrew Buncombe and Tessa MacArthur

Within the boundaries of the capital, 300 different languages are regularly spoken. 'London is clearly the most cosmopolitan city in Europe and only New York can claim to be as world class in terms of its internationalism,' said Patrick Kerr, a spokesman for London First, Greater London's inward investment agency. Such diversity has a range of benefits. Mr Kerr said the language pool was a major attraction for companies operating within the global market.

Most reports into the number of languages spoken in London are based on research carried out in 1993 by the University of London's School of Oriental and African Studies. This research estimated that 275 languages were regularly spoken within the capital. However, *The Independent* has learnt that new research will reveal a total that is closer to 300.

London's linguistic diversity is matched by the breadth of its ethnic make-up. Figures collated by the London Research Centre show that there are 33 communities of more than 10,000 people who were born outside of England. There are a further 12 communities of more than 5,000. These groups range from those born in Ireland, who number more than 200,000 to the Mauritian community, which numbers around 14,000.

Extract from *The Independent*, 29 March 1999

## TASKS

1. A recent survey showed people believe that 26 per cent of the population belong to a minority ethnic group. What is the actual figure?
2. In what ways is immigration helpful to the UK economy?
3. Of the 4 million people in the UK who were born elsewhere, how many are white? How many are from other ethnic groups? Do you think this fits people's expectations?
4. What is the total membership of Christian churches in the UK?
5. The number of people from different ethnic backgrounds is one indicator of a multicultural society. What other signs are there that Britain is a multicultural society?
6. Make up your own quick quiz to ask people. Base the questions on the information that you can find. For example:
   (a) what percentage of the population belongs to an ethnic minority, or
   (b) how many Muslims are there in the UK?

## TAKING THIS FURTHER

Carry out a survey of your school or local community. What diversity of language, religion or ethnic background can you find? How does this compare with the national figures? Is your school or area typical?

What other types of diversity can you find? List the ways in which this diversity makes your school or area a better place.

# Respecting diversity

**We have many points in common with some people – from our nationality, race, sex and age to personal interests or religion. But of course these similarities also make us different from other people.**

## The same but different

It is easy to respect other people when they agree with us. It is a real test of our **tolerance** when other people's lives are very different from ours or if they strongly disagree with us. The United Nations recognised, when it was discussing people's rights, that one of the most important rights is to be different from each other and to be respected as an individual. The Universal Declaration of Human Rights clearly states that we all:

Article 1: are free and that we should be treated in the same way

Article 2: are equal despite differences in skin, colour, sex, religion and language

Article 18: have the right to practise and observe all aspects of our religion

Article 27: have the right to celebrate our culture and customs.

a) Jaspreet would like to celebrate the birth of Guru Nanak, an important person in the religion she believes in. However, the day of the celebrations is a school day. Her parents are happy for her to take the day off school so she can go to the temple, but her school is not happy for her to have time off for a religious celebration.

b) Ruth and David both work for a bank in the city. Ruth has been working at the bank for eight years, she is very experienced and has a lot of responsibility. She is in charge of ten employees. David has been working for the bank for five years, he has not got as much experience and is not in charge of anybody. The Board of Directors of the bank have decided to promote David above Ruth and pay him a higher salary because they feel he will bring more customers to the bank and give it a more dynamic image.

c) Catherine has recently moved to England from France. She can understand English but finds it difficult to communicate. Some of the teachers in the school she attends feel that she should not be in the same classes as the other pupils of her age until her language has improved.

d) Shabana is a Muslim and has always worn a headscarf at school. Recently she has asked permission to wear a full-length covering which would cover her whole head and body. She feels this is an important part of following her religion in the way she wants. The school has denied her permission saying that the covering is not part of school uniform.

### TASK

**1** Look at the Human Rights Articles, read descriptions a) to d) above, then complete the following table:

| Brief description of the scenario | Which article is the scenario referring to? | Is the article being respected? | Possible solution |
|---|---|---|---|
| | | | |
| | | | |
| | | | |
| | | | |

# Living together

**Living in a multicultural society means that there are many different customs governing our behaviour. In different religions and cultures people's ideas about what makes someone a good person and what makes a good life vary. This means we have different ideas about how people should live their lives.**

We need a fair set of rules and laws to live by so that everyone has their rights recognised and is free to live their life as they want. This often leads to problems as groups argue over what should and should not be allowed. Some people have tried to draw up rules to help us deal with such arguments. Below are some ideas from the writings of John Stuart Mill, who wrote and worked as an MP over 100 years ago.

'If all mankind minus one were of one opinion, mankind would be no more justified in silencing that one person than he, if he had the power, would be justified in silencing mankind.'

'The liberty of the individual should only be limited by this; he should not interfere in other people's lives. If he leaves other people to make their own decisions and to believe what they want, then he should have the same freedom to do and believe what he wants.'

'It would not be beneficial if everyone agreed on everything. Diversity is not an evil, but a good. As it is useful that there should be different opinions, it is also important that there should be different experiments in living. When people are free to pursue their own lives in their own ways they are more likely to be happy.'

'Society should be able to interfere with an individual's freedom only if people use their freedom to harm the interests of others. Any legal action should be guided by the desire to improve the situation overall and protect people's rights.'

Adapted from John Stuart Mill, *On Liberty*, 1859

## TASKS

**1** Do you have an opinion about one of the cases from page 20 which you know a friend or someone in your class disagrees with?
- (a) Describe what your point of view is.
- (b) Why does the other person disagree with your opinion?
- (c) What is their opinion?
- (d) Why don't you agree with their point of view?

**2** Is it important for people to have their own opinions about different issues? Give reasons for your answer.

**3** Look at John Stuart Mill's ideas:
- (a) Can you think of how the situation could be solved if people followed these rules?
- (b) Can you think of a situation that might not be so easily solved?

**4** What would it be like if people's differences were not respected in:
- (a) your school?
- (b) your community?
- (c) your country?

**5** Do you agree with Mill's ideas?

# One system for all?

## Where do you stand?

Look at the following cases, which are **controversial** and require you to think about the people involved, their rights and the nature of diversity in society.

### Case 1: Freedom of Speech?

In 1988 Salman Rushdie wrote a book called *The Satanic Verses*. It was about a fictional prophet who starts his own religion. It was based on aspects of the life of the prophet Mohammed, who founded the religion of Islam. Many Muslims were very offended by the way Rushdie appeared to be making fun of Mohammed's life and his disrespectful attitude towards their religion. In 1989 an Iranian religious leader, the Ayatollah Khomeini, passed a death sentence on Rushdie and called on Muslims to kill him. The Khordad Foundation offered a reward to the killer of $1 million, which was increased later to $2.5 million. Salman Rushdie went into hiding and has had protection from the British police since 1989. In the meantime, bookshops in the UK and USA have been bombed, books have been burned in public, Rushdie's Norwegian publisher was shot and seriously injured, the Italian translator was attacked and the Japanese translator was killed.

1. Should Salman Rushdie have written the book?
2. Should he have been allowed to publish it?
3. Were those who took action against him and others involved with the book justified?

### Case 2: Religious Freedom?

The Jewish Sabbath runs from Friday evening to Saturday evening and Jews who follow it strictly do not drive cars, cook, or carry any articles in the street, which includes the pushing of prams. An *eruv* is a traditional enclosed area that is considered part of the home and therefore enables Jews to go about their neighbourhood more freely with prams on the Sabbath. There are *eruvs* all over the world from Australia to America. Since 1991, a number of Jews in North London have been trying to get permission to establish an *eruv* in their neighbourhood, which would involve putting up 85 poles and 1.2 miles of wire around their local area. The council postponed a decision on this request for nine years but has finally agreed in principle to allow the Jews to build the fences. Other residents have argued that the boundary **discriminates** against other people's rights as everyone in the neighbourhood would have to go through the gateways, even if they are not Jewish themselves.

1. Should the Jewish community be allowed to put up their boundary to establish the *eruv*?
2. Should other residents be allowed to stop them?

### Case 3: Freedom of Choice?

During the 1950s some pubs and bed-and-breakfast houses used to put up cards in their windows saying 'No Blacks, No Irish'. This is now illegal and laws make it clear that it is unacceptable to discriminate against people on the basis of their race or ethnicity. Some pubs today have new signs in the windows saying 'No travellers, No football colours, No site clothes'.

1. Can pub landlords refuse to serve people they do not want in their pub?
2. Pub landlords may refuse to serve supporters in football colours in case they cause trouble, and workers in site clothes because they are likely to be dirty. Why would they want to ban travellers as well?
3. Should landlords have the right to ban travellers?
4. Should travellers have the same rights as ethnic minorities?

### Case 4: Freedom from Discrimination?

In 1998 Lisa Grant and Jill Percy took South West Trains to court for discriminating against them. The train company usually offers free or cheap transport to the partners of their heterosexual employees. But Lisa and Jill, who were long-term partners, were not allowed to have the same arrangement as other couples. In court they argued that discriminating against them on the grounds that they were lesbians was as bad as discriminating against them because they were women, and effectively was no different. At the time it was legal to discriminate against people because of their sexuality, but not because of their sex. The Human Rights Act may change this.

1. Should South West Trains be able to decide who qualifies for such a deal?
2. Should a gay relationship be recognised as equal to a straight one in this case?
3. Should there be any differences at all in the way the law treats people on the grounds of their relationship?

### Case 5: Freedom to Meet?

There has been a relatively high number of asylum seekers arriving in Kent, especially in Dover, for a number of years. Supporters of far-right groups, such as the British National Party and others, have marched on several occasions to protest against the number of **immigrants** in the UK and to argue for tougher asylum laws. Local protestors argue that such groups are openly racist and should not be allowed to march. These locals always far outnumber the marchers. They say that no one should have the freedom to be racist and that when the far right is allowed to march it encourages others to be more openly racist. The marchers say they have a right to meet and campaign just like everyone else. Local police have to protect everyone's rights and they monitor what the marchers do and say to make sure they do not break the law. Whilst they stay within the law, the police protect their right to march.

1. What effect do you think racist marches have on the public?
2. Should the far-right marchers be stopped from campaigning?
3. Should the police protect them from the anti-fascist campaigners?

## TASKS

**1** Describe your initial reaction to the individual cases.

**2** For each of the cases who do you think is in the 'right' and who is in the 'wrong'?

**3** Choose one example and write two articles, one for the case and one against the case. Remember to give reasons for the point of view you are representing.

**4** What action would you recommend to promote a tolerant society?

**5** Do Mill's ideas help with any of these issues?

# The Arms Trade

**One of the main jobs of any government is to defend its country and people. To do this effectively governments have to maintain armed forces including the army, air force and navy. Large amounts of money need to be spent, even in times of peace, to keep people employed in these services, to update their equipment, and to research into new technology.**

## SKILLS FOCUS

- Thinking about different views and developing your own opinions

From the 1950s to the 1990s there was an 'arms race', a situation in which the USA and USSR (now Russia) continued to build up more and more nuclear weapons so that their weapons would not be outnumbered by those of the other country. This made many people scared that a nuclear war might break out. It also meant that the two governments spent huge amounts of money on nuclear weapons and other arms. This Cold War, as it became known, led to the arms industry becoming one of the biggest in the world, second only to oil.

## USEFUL WORDS

**Civilians** – people not in the armed services or police

**Adversary** – enemy or opponent

**Ethical** – morally correct

**Repression** – keep under control, often with force

**Dictator** – a single person ruling a whole country, usually not elected

## TASKS

1. Can you find examples of changes in the arms trade?
2. Are there any facts about these changes that surprise you?
3. Are some countries more important in the arms trade than others?
4. Find an example of one government encouraging another to spend more on arms.
5. Find an example of a government controlling sales to another.

### FACT 1

Between 1945 and 1992 there were 149 major wars throughout the world, killing more than 23 million people.

### FACT 2

| Top Arms Companies | |
|---|---|
| *Company* | *Arms sales (US$ billion)* |
| BAE Systems | 19.0 |
| Lockheed Martin | 17.8 |
| Boeing | 16.3 |
| Raytheon | 14.5 |
| General Dynamics | 9.0 |
| EADS | 6.1 |
| Northrop Grumman | 6.0 |
| Thales (then Thomson-CSF) | 3.6 |

### FACT 3

In 1993, at the end of the Cold War, there were 42 countries involved in 52 major conflicts. There was political violence in a further 37 countries.

**FACT 4**

Of the 23 million people killed in wars since the end of the Second World War and the end of the Cold War, more than half were civilians.

**FACT 5**

One present-day nuclear submarine carries eight times the amount of fire power used in the whole of the Second World War.

**FACT 6**

Even after the Cold War, the USA and Russia remained the biggest manufacturers of weapons. India was the biggest buyer.

**FACT 7**

There are estimated to be 30 million landmines spread across 18 countries in Africa.

**FACT 8**

Producing one landmine costs as little as £2. Getting rid of it safely can cost between £200 and £500.

**FACT 9**

The overwhelming majority of armed conflicts are not between states but within them.

**FACT 10**

In 1998 the US government gave $3.2 billion in military aid to several countries, to be spent on US arms. The largest amounts were $1.8 billion to Israel and $1.3 billion to Egypt.

**FACT 11**

In 1999 Malaysia was the UK arms industry's biggest customer. The UK government gave permission for British companies to sell £495 million worth of military goods to the Malaysian government. The UK government refused permission to 130 requests from defence companies for licences to sell arms in that year.

**FACT 12**

The 1997 international agreement, the 'Ottawa Convention', bans the use, stockpiling, production and transfer of anti-personnel mines and recommends their destruction. It came into operation on 1 March 1999. The Landmines Act in the UK makes it a criminal offence to use, develop, produce, keep, trade or transfer an anti-personnel landmine.

**FACT 13**

Towards the end of the Cold War, the USA was spending $400 billion per year on defence. By the end of the 1990s that figure was slightly less than $300 billion.

**FACT 14**

More than 500 million small arms and light weapons are in circulation around the world – one for about every 12 people. They were the weapons of choice in 46 out of 49 major conflicts since 1990, causing 4 million deaths – about 90 per cent of them civilians, of whom 80 per cent were women and children.

**FACT 15**

An estimated 50 to 60 per cent of the world's trade of small arms is legal.

**FACT 16**

In 1999 global military spending was approximately $780 billion. This sum is about 30 per cent less than the total in 1990, but it is a 2 per cent increase on the figure for 1998.

# Opinions about the Arms Trade

**Defence is important and every country, whether it is rich or poor, has a right to defend itself. Does that mean every country has a right to buy whatever weapons it wants?**

### TASK

Look at the opinions and comments on these pages and try to summarise the reasoning behind each one. You could present your results in a table like the one below:

| Source | Description | Opinion |
|---|---|---|
| A | *Grid showing military spending and alternatives* | *I think the person who produced this disapproved of the arms trade because they focus on all the practical and helpful things governments could do with the money they spend on the military.* |
| | | |

**World military spending and its alternatives**

**A**

This diagram was produced in 1992. What has happened since then to the total amount of military spending?

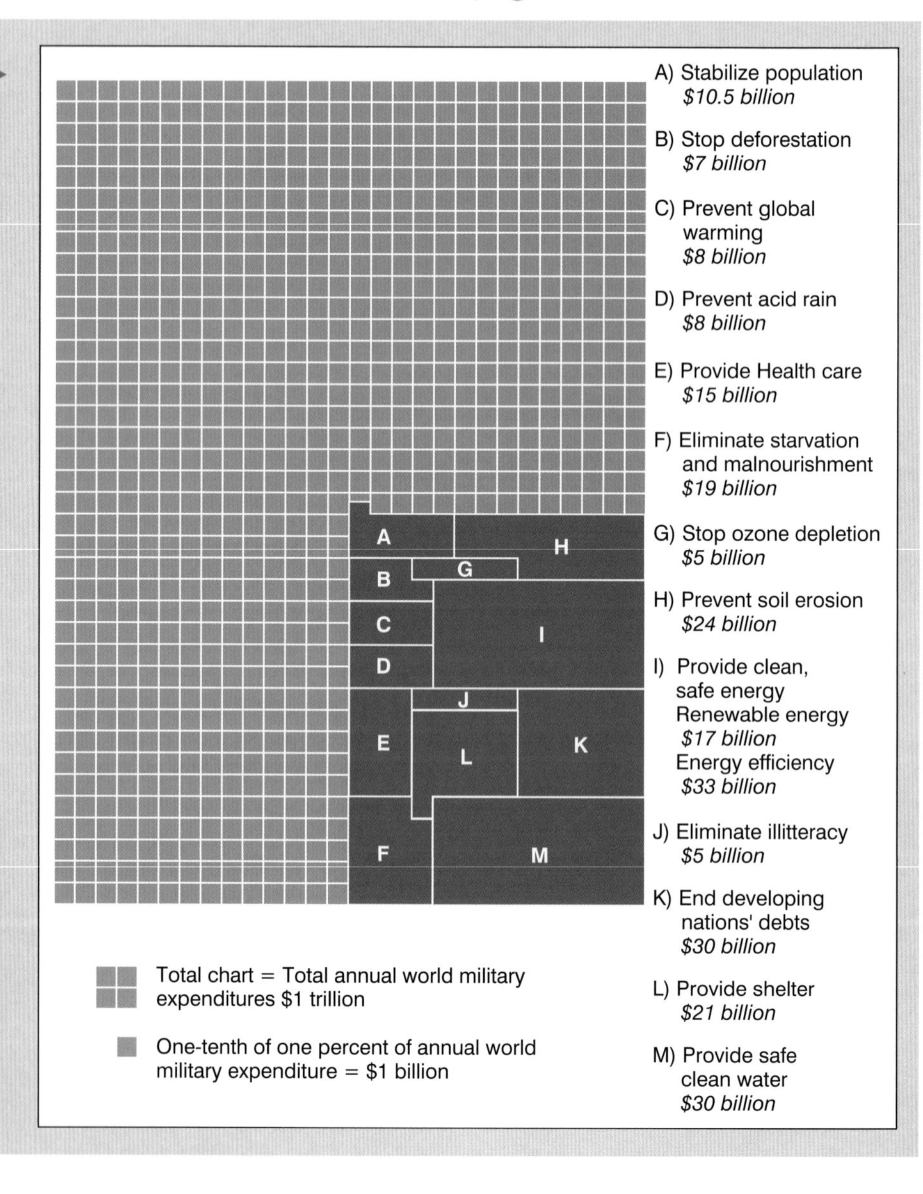

**B**

'"We have an overwhelming advantage over any potential **adversary**," said the then Defence Secretary William Cohen early in 1999. "We like that and want to keep it" (*Financial Times*, 2 February 1999). More recently he told US businessmen that 'US economic power is still dependent on military strength and a strong defence industry' – or, as one expert has more bluntly put it: "behind the hidden hand of the market is a hidden fist" (Thomas Friedman, quoted in Foreign Policy in Focus policy report, 24 April 2000).'

Extract from 'The Arms Industry' by Christopher Wrigley, March 2001

**C**

All governments are hypocritical about the arms trade. They keep business out of the public eye whilst selling as much as they possibly can. Controls such as the United Nations Conventional Arms Register* could work but only if governments were willing to admit what they have been selling. However, many buyers want to keep their purchases secret and suppliers have to agree or they may lose their contracts.

Adapted from an interview with an arms dealer in *The New Internationalist*, November 1994

* When the Register was introduced in 1992 almost all exporters listed what they were selling but over 60 per cent of importers refused to do so.

**D**

**E**

INTERVIEWER:
'Is the whole **ethical** foreign policy beginning to unravel? Can we start with Indonesia? Why are we still selling military equipment to them?'

FOREIGN SECRETARY:
'Sadly, it does appear to be the case that some of the equipment being used against these rioters are sold from Britain. They would, of course, not have been sold under the new criteria that we have brought in and under which we have refused seven applications from Indonesia for the type of equipment that the previous Government did sell. There has been a big difference in what we would sell and we have made it quite clear we will not sell equipment that will be used in internal repression.'

Extract from interview given by the Foreign Secretary, Robin Cook, for BBC radio, 14 May 1998

**F**

'We see several possibilities such as the sale of Hawk fighter jets and Scorpion light tanks and other equipment ... It is not for me to get involved in the politics of another country. Quite clearly it is an issue that concerns some but what I am concerned with is the working relationship between the armed forces of Britain and Indonesia.'

British Chief of Defence Staff, Field Marshall Peter Inge, 1994

**G**

During the years 1987–94, the industrial nations appear to have saved $810 billion, and the developing nations $125 billion, producing a sizeable peace dividend of $935 billion. But it is difficult to track where these funds went. Most of the savings appear to have been spent on reducing countries' debts rather than spending on social or environmental improvements.

Adapted from the Human Development Report, 1994 (UN Development Programme)

# Who should Britain trade arms with?

**The British government does not allow British companies to sell to whoever wants to buy their products. Companies must apply for a licence for each deal they make with a foreign government. The British government gives permission if it believes the goods sold will not be used for aggression against other countries, or to control people within the country.**

The government aims to sell products which are mainly used for defence but this is often more difficult to decide than it sounds. The same equipment can be used for different purposes and what may be sold for one reason may end up being used for another. If a government buys tanks to defend its country against an aggressive neighbour, it is possible that they can be used to intimidate its own citizens.

Below are three possible case studies that a British government official might have to make a decision about. In each case decide whether you would grant the licence, refuse it, or allow only part of the deal to go ahead.

### Case Study 1

Twigland has had a good relationship with Britain since the end of the Second World War. Twigland's government has bought much of its weaponry from British manufacturers over the last 50 years and there are hundreds of British workers who help Twigland's military to maintain the equipment it has bought. Twigland is now looking to buy six new air-to-ground missile launchers (£5 million) and a number of spare parts for previous purchases (£2.5 million). Reports from British staff in the country have recently indicated that one of Twigland's neighbours is seeking to take some of its territory to the north. Twigland is a democracy and all elections in the last 20 years were peaceful.

### Case Study 2

Leafland has suffered from an on-going civil war for the past 25 years. The south of the country has long been the stronghold of the Leafland government, led by a military **dictator**. Over the past 18 months, his armed forces have taken over almost all of the northern half of the country and he claims he is about to finally defeat the opposition and unite the country once and for all. His government is going to spend £35 million on tanks, jeeps and personnel carriers. There is a military-vehicle manufacturer in the north of the UK on the verge of closure through lack of orders, and unless they win this contract they will have to make 300 people redundant.

### Case Study 3

Forestria is a democracy but has kept the same party in government for the last 30 years. It is hoping to buy 10 tanks (£20 million), 7 new jet fighters (£25 million), radar equipment and aircraft (£15 million) and long-distance anti-tank missiles (£10 million). There has been a recent change in party leader and the new man has already banned newspapers of minority cultural groups and postponed the next election. Forestria has good relationships with several other countries who could each provide some of the equipment the Forestrian government is requesting.

## TASKS

1 In groups of 3 or 4 discuss the decisions you made about who should be able to trade with Britain. Share your reasons and see if you can reach agreement.

2 Below are three factors that a government might choose to consider when reaching such a decision. Copy them into your notes. Then think of as many additional factors as you can and write them down as well.

Is the government likely to use the goods they buy to attack another country?

How will the sale affect the arms industry in Britain? Will it safeguard jobs? What would be the impact if the sale were not allowed?

Is there any international agreement not to arm this country?

3 What are the most important factors that the government should think about?

4 Some people would like to ban the arms trade. Others argue that it is an important trade to continue with. Copy the table below and make a list of points for and against banning the arms trade.

5 Prepare for a class discussion about 'Britain's Attitude Towards the Arms Trade'. You could do some further research to find out more about the people with whom Britain trades and the ways in which arms trading has changed over the years. Think about your opinion and try to come up with as many reasons as you can to support your position.

6 Draw up some guidelines that you think the government should stick to when selling arms.

What kinds of arms should it sell and what should it never sell?

What checks could it carry out before selling arms?

Are there some other types of governments who should be favoured?

Are there other countries that should not be sold arms?

What purposes is it acceptable to sell arms for?

| Reasons to continue the arms trade | Reasons to stop the arms trade |
|---|---|
| *Each country needs to able to get hold of the best weapons to defend itself.* | *It is wrong to make a profit from selling weapons when you know how harmful they are.* |
| | |

### TAKING IT FURTHER

**Research**

Why not find out more about the countries that Britain has been selling arms to. You will see from the evidence in this chapter that there have been some important changes in policy over the past few years. It is also easier to find out information about Britain's arms trade than ever before. You might want to look at one country that has bought arms and find out about the situation in that country. According to your guidelines should the arms sale have gone ahead?

### ACTION

Think about the kinds of action ordinary citizens can take in relation to the arms trade. Investigate the groups who campaign on arms. You could also look at decisions that people make about ethical investment. Some people make decisions about where to invest their money or save for their pension, based on what the money is invested in. Some banks offer services that never invest in the arms trade. Where can you find out about such companies? Would you worry about this if you were investing money?

# Who runs the world?

**National governments are responsible for defence, keeping law and order, enforcing rules about fair trade, providing some level of healthcare and helping to meet other basic needs such as housing, education and income. At the global level, whilst there is no single government providing all of these, there are various organisations and institutions that exist to carry out some of these actions across country borders and in some cases all over the world.**

## Investigation

The rest of this chapter gives you some basic information to get started on a research project to find out what global institutions there are that affect people's lives across the world. There is one page on each of five different organisations or groups and each one is intended as a basic introduction. You must do some more detailed investigation yourself to become a specialist in one of those areas.

### USEFUL WORDS

**Equitable** – fair and more equal

**Intervene** – get involved in a conflict, between the two sides

**Demobilisation** – the end of armed force: sending all the soldiers back home and taking their weapons from them

**Corporation** – a business, company

**Consumption** – the quantity of products and natural resources being used up

### SKILLS FOCUS

- Group work and presentation skills
- Justifying and discussing opinions

At the back of this book there is a selection of web links for this chapter to give you some additional ideas as starting points.

*"If we act now with realism and foresight,*
*if we show courage,*
*if we think globally and*
*allocate our resources accordingly,*
*we can give our children a*
*more peaceful and* ***equitable*** *world.*
*One where suffering will be reduced.*
*Where children everywhere*
*Will have a sense of hope.*
*This is not just a dream.*
*It is our responsibility."*

James D. Wolfenson, President of the World Bank

### TASKS

1. Split the class into five groups. Each group should take one page as a starting point for their research.
2. Read through and discuss the information on the page. You should present your research into your topic and describe how important and powerful your organisation or group is in the world. You should also talk about how democratic your organisation is.
3. Once you have discussed the topic you will have to decide how you are going to present your case to the rest of the class. Will you produce leaflets, a book, a video, tape recording, drama, documentary, news report, or computer presentation? Each type of presentation may require different skills so make sure you discuss what team members are good at before you decide what you will produce.
4. Draw up a timetable for work and allocate roles to the group members. What needs to be done in order to be finished on time? Who needs to do what and by when?
5. For research you may find newspapers particularly useful. If you can access the Internet, the following websites have very good search engines in an archive section: www.guardian.co.uk or www.thetimes.co.uk.
6. After each presentation, discuss with the research group what they found most important about their organisation. Think for yourself – how important does each institution seem to you? You could give each of them a power rating from 1 to 5, to compare them at the end of the presentations.

REMEMBER

This activity will be as much a test of your skills of research and working with others as it will be about what you know about your topic.

# United Nations

### Aims

The United Nations (UN) has four purposes:

- To maintain international peace and security
- To develop friendly relations among nations
- To cooperate in solving international problems and in promoting respect for human rights
- To be a centre for harmonising the actions of nations.

### Membership

Membership now totals 189 countries – almost every country in the world.

### Activities

The UN has six main parts, each of which carries out its own activities:

- General Assembly – provides a forum for all 189 members to meet and discuss issues. The General Assembly can make decisions but they are not binding on members, they merely give advice on how to act.
- Security Council – Britain, France, the USA, Russia and China are the permanent members of the Security Council. They are joined by ten other countries, which are elected by the General Assembly for two years at a time. The Security Council decides on all security matters and can authorise armed peacekeeping forces to **intervene** in conflicts.
- Economic and Social Council – this has 54 members, each serving for three years. It also has several organisations within it with responsibility for specific issues such as refugees, human rights, natural resources and women's position in society.
- Trusteeship Council – in the past, this part of the UN took responsibility for protecting small countries that were no longer colonies but were not yet fully independent. In 1994, the last country, Palau, became independent and the Council now meets very rarely.
- Secretariat – this is the central staff of the UN. The Secretariat is led by the Secretary General, who is elected for 5-year terms by the Security Council.
- International Court of Justice – this is made up of 15 judges elected for 9-year periods by the Security Council and the General Assembly. It aims to resolve disagreements and enforce international law.

### Successes

In 1989, in Nicaragua, the UN's peace effort led to the voluntary **demobilisation** of the resistance movement, whose members turned in their weapons to the UN.

During 1999, combined UN appeals raised more than $1.4 billion for emergency humanitarian assistance to help 26 million people.

### Weaknesses

The UN is dependent on the contributions paid to it by member states for funding its activities. Some of the members only pay some of the money owed to the UN, therefore it is not always possible for the UN to act.

The Security Council is dominated by five permanent members who often disagree on fundamental issues and therefore hold up action.

### TASKS

1 List five current issues in which you think the UN would be able to become involved.

2 In each of those situations what could the UN do to solve the problems?

3 (a) What are the main strengths of the UN?
(b) Are there any negative effects of the UN?

4 What are the similarities and differences between governments and the UN?

# The World Bank and the International Monetary Fund

## Aims

The World Bank and the International Monetary Fund (IMF) were both established at the end of the Second World War as a result of the Bretton Woods Conference. The World Bank was originally intended to provide loans to European countries rebuilding their economies after the war. Eventually it made more loans to developing countries to help them with their development plans. The IMF was started to help keep currencies stable around the world and make trade easier.

## Membership

The World Bank has 183 member countries, each of which is also a member of the IMF. The countries all own shares in the Bank and each country has one governor. The governors meet once a year to decide the Bank's policy and review membership. In between the annual meetings, most decisions are made by the Board of Executive Directors. France, Germany, Japan, the UK and the USA all appoint one executive director, and all the other 178 countries elect 19 directors between them.

## Activities

The World Bank promotes economic development through loans, while the IMF encourages trade and a stable world economy and also provides short-term loans to allow governments to manage their currencies. Although each of the organisations has a separate focus, they often work closely together.

Poorer countries are often reliant on World Bank and IMF support. Critics of the two institutions point out that this means that they can have too much power over governments. If a government wants to borrow money, it has to agree to the suggestions of the World Bank and IMF about how its economy should be run and how the money should be spent.

Recently the two organisations have begun to cancel the debts of some of the poorest and most indebted countries. This means that those countries will have a better chance of developing their economies because they will not have to repay so much in interest charges (see Chapter 9, on the debt crisis).

## Successes

Both organisations have been able to help countries in need of money by providing loans. The World Bank helps to fund projects which are intended to develop poorer countries' economies.

They stop countries from going bankrupt.

The World Bank is the world's largest funder (outside of government) of education and health.

## Weaknesses

The main criticism is that the World Bank and IMF are more interested in money than people.

Many of the loans are criticised because they are for funding large projects such as dams, which can be very disruptive for the lives of ordinary people.

Critics also argue that the World Bank and IMF have too much power over the decisions of governments. They say that the rules forced on borrowers are often destructive – for example, opening up a national economy to world trade even though foreign producers can sell the goods more cheaply. This means the World Bank has more influence in making decisions about trade policy, government spending and work law than a country's own elected government.

## TASKS

1 List three situations in which the World Bank or IMF might become involved.

2 In each of your examples, what could they do to improve the situation?

3 (a) What are the main strengths of the World Bank and IMF?
(b) What negative effects might they have?

4 What are the similarities and differences between governments and the World Bank and IMF?

# Multinational corporations

### Aims

Like all businesses, the main aim of multinational **corporations** is to make a profit. Multinationals vary in the extent to which they also follow other aims such as protecting workers' rights, paying fair wages and protecting the environment.

### Countries affected

Multinational corporations affect every country in the world. They run offices, manufacture goods or just sell their products and services everywhere.

### Activities

Multinational corporations are businesses that operate in not just one but several countries. They are involved in every type of activity from farming, mining and producing and operating computers to providing legal and financial advice and services. Manufacturing companies often find it especially useful to operate around the world as some countries offer them specific advantages.

*Example: the textile industry has become largely international and it is common for designs to be created in richer countries, whilst clothes are actually made in poorer countries where wages are lower. The clothes can then be sold in the richer countries where people have more money to spend.*

In 1998, the world's five largest companies achieved sales higher than the incomes of the poorest 46 countries combined. The increasing freedom of world trade means that companies can move goods and money wherever they want. Some people argue that this means multinational corporations are now more powerful and influential than many governments, because they are not controlled by national borders.

### Successes

Companies operating internationally create jobs all around the world thus spreading skills and technology to all countries.

Large wealthy corporations can work together with poor governments to help the latter plan for development and improve their people's standard of living.

Some multinational corporations want to protect the environment and are so powerful they can make a noticeable improvement quite easily.

### Weaknesses

Some countries are so keen to attract multinational companies that they set up special areas for them in which to produce their goods. Here the multinationals pay low taxes, often have cheaper power and pay low wages. This means that local people gain employment but the government receives few other benefits.

If workers join together to demand better conditions it is sometimes easier for a multinational company to move its production elsewhere rather than meet their demands, leaving the people with no jobs. The most extreme companies put up portable factories in order to discourage workers from complaining.

*"To attract companies like yours … we have felled mountains, razed jungles, filled swamps, moved rivers, relocated towns … all to make it easier for you and your business to do business here".*

Extract from an advertisement placed by the Philippine government in *Fortune* magazine, 1971

## TASKS

1. List the ways in which multinational corporations can influence people's lives around the world.
   (a) How could multinationals improve people's lives?
   (b) What negative effects might they have?
2. What are the similarities and differences between governments and multinationals?
3. What role do multinational companies have in influencing how the world is run?

# World Trade Organisation

## Aims

The World Trade Organisation (WTO) exists to make sure member countries obey a common set of rules to help make trade flow around the world as smoothly as possible and to allow countries to compete freely with each other.

## Membership

By the end of the year 2000 there were 139 members of the WTO and 30 countries waiting to join.

## Activities

The Ministerial Conference meets at least once every two years to make major decisions. Day-to-day decisions are taken by the General Council, which meets to settle disputes between members and review the trade policy of members' states. There are also other councils and committees to consider individual areas of trade such as intellectual property, trade in services and the environment. Panels of experts are set up to decide individual disputes brought to the WTO.

Decisions are supposed to be reached by consensus – that means everyone should come to an agreement. Where this is impossible, a majority can make decisions. When one member believes another is acting unfairly or breaking the rules they can take their case to the WTO and both members are bound to accept and act on its decision.

## Successes

The WTO requires countries to open up their economies to world trade. This increases competition, forces countries to develop efficient industries and leads to lower prices. It also means that poorer countries are able to export their goods to richer countries and earn more money.

In one dispute between the USA and the EU, the USA complained that the EU was discriminating against banana-growers in Latin America by allowing more bananas to be imported from the Caribbean. The WTO said this was unfair and told the EU to treat both sets of countries equally.

## Weaknesses

In the above case, the EU argued that it had taken more bananas from the Caribbean banana-growers because it was trying to help those countries improve their economies – selling to the EU would boost their income. By deciding against the EU, the WTO has stopped it from helping countries through trading decisions.

Some critics argue that the current rules of the WTO are not very helpful to poorer countries as they are less likely to have strong industries that could compete in the world market. The WTO is also more likely to come under pressure from powerful governments to vote how those governments want, in exchange for favours later.

Expert panels report in secret, but their decisions are binding on governments.

Some people are concerned about the ways in which the WTO might decide to influence trade. In trying to make sure that there are fewer barriers to free trade, critics argue that the WTO may be ignoring some other factors that are also important. For example, a country might decide it wants to import tuna caught in nets which do not trap dolphins. This makes the tuna more expensive than tuna caught in traditional nets. The WTO is the organisation that would have to decide whether it was legal for a country to discriminate in favour of one provider over another.

## TASKS

1 What is the WTO for?

2 How is it supposed to solve problems?

3 (a) What are the main strengths and advantages of the WTO?
(b) What negative effects might the WTO cause?

4 What are the similarities and differences between governments and the WTO?

# Non-Governmental Organisations

### Aims

Every Non-Governmental Organisation (NGO) has its own aims but many share some similarities (see Chapter 6, Voluntary Groups). In 1992, thousands of NGOs met to agree a Declaration of Common Principles. Among other matters, they agreed to promote putting basic needs before profit, controlling **consumption** as well as population, putting individuals before the interests of companies and encouraging everyone to get involved in their communities.

### Countries affected

NGOs are established in every country and many work across boundaries. Increasingly, the Internet helps them to work with each other around the world.

### Activities

The following list highlights some of the actions NGOs have undertaken around the world.

- Providing a network to allow farmers in developing countries to contact each other.
- Meeting with multinational corporations to convince them to improve the way they work around the world.
- Organising marches and demonstrations against the WTO, World Bank and IMF to put pressure on them to adopt policies which do not harm the world's poor and and which protect the environment.
- Collecting and distributing money to help those most in need.
- Researching the effects of chemicals and manufacturing on the environment.
- Working with and advising the WTO, World Bank and IMF to help them develop projects in the interests of people around the world.
- Organising petitions to support their aims.
- Working directly with communities to help them develop their capacity to improve their own lives.
- Campaigning to get prisoners of conscience released.

### Successes

Many international institutions now recognise the expertise of NGOs and often work with people from NGO backgrounds to plan useful development projects.

In 1999, at the WTO meeting in Seattle, NGOs helped to bring together 50,000 protestors to show the WTO that ordinary people from all over the world were worried by what it was doing. This contributed to the meeting being postponed and assurances from governments that they would listen more carefully to the people.

### Weaknesses

NGOs are often reliant on charitable donations.

Governments and multinational companies have access to expensive media and public-relations projects to promote their activities. NGOs are often much poorer and have to rely on other methods to get their messages heard.

### TASKS

1. List five current issues in which an NGO would become involved.
2. Which NGO would be most appropriate for each of those issues and what might they do to solve the problems?
3. Give an example of a situation in which an NGO might be better suited to take action than a government.
4. (a) What are the main strengths of NGOs?
   (b) What negative effects might NGOs have?
5. Would the world work without NGOs?

# Action without borders

▲1

▲2

▲3

▲4

▲5

**Do you recognise any of the emblems?**
**Some are more familiar than others, but there is something that links all these organisations together – they are all Non-Governmental Organisations (NGOs).**

### SKILLS FOCUS

- Think about the role of NGOs and understand the situations in which governments are unable to act

## What does this mean?

These organisations do not belong to nor are they linked with a government. They are independent, non-profit-making organisations. There are thousands of NGOs, both in developed and developing countries. They provide a range of services and support from funding the activities of volunteers to educating people. They often work towards peace, environmental protection, human rights, fair wages, justice, health and sustainable development.

As with any sector there are differences in approach amongst NGOs:

**The Welfare Approach**
Providing relief: for example, food aid, medical assistance, refugee support, transport, etc.

**The Developmental Approach**
Providing support to local groups for projects in education, health, agriculture, medicine, housing, literacy, etc.

**The Empowerment Approach**
Usually more political projects including training local leaders, defending human rights, encouraging real participation, challenging injustice, racism, etc.

**The Education or Campaigning Approach**
Promoting educational projects in the developed world, aimed at highlighting our responsibilities to people in other countries or those less well off than ourselves.

Some NGOs make use of all of these approaches, while others may overlap two or more.

## But there is a need for politics

Some people argue that charities should just concentrate on helping people but in practice, all charities have to have a political side to them. On the simplest level, a charity concerned with single parents, for example, has to be able to speak out against a government that reduces welfare payments for this group. Any agency concerned with development in the third world has to speak up against the forces that stop people having a chance for a better quality of life. People who object to organisations taking a political stand are always free to withhold their donations if they do not agree with what a NGO says or does.

### USEFUL WORDS

**Neutral** – not taking sides

**Liaison** – communication or cooperation

**Alleviate** – make something less severe or less painful

**Voluntary service** – giving your time for free

**Solidarity** – unity, being together and supporting each other

## TASKS

1 Why do you think it is important for NGOs to be independent of government control?

2 Look at the NGO logos at the top of page 36. What kind of work does each organisation undertake? Which approach, or approaches, best describe each NGO?

3 There are a number of characteristics of NGOs which highlight the difference between them and governments. There are also advantages and disadvantages to NGOs. Organise the statements (a) to (k) below into the following two groups:

Advantages of NGOs
Disadvantages of NGOs.

(a) They can bypass governments and get more directly in touch with local people and their needs. This is very important when governments are not representative or are involved in conflicts.

(b) NGOs often represent the needs and views of people in the developed rather than the developing worlds.

(c) The scale of their work is tiny by comparison with the scale of the problems.

(d) NGOs can work in situations where governments, because of their involvement in international politics, cannot.

(e) Often NGOs are based on a 'do-gooder' philosophy, and therefore can be ineffective or unprofessional and fail to address the real issues.

(f) Because NGOs are usually small in scale, large or inappropriate projects are often avoided.

(g) NGOs can work for political change in the developed world. They can openly challenge injustice and inequality – for example, the Drop the Debt campaign.

(i) They are frequently faced with the dilemma of fundraising and they often use 'starving baby' images to make their appeals, rather than a more balanced and accurate presentation of developing countries.

(j) NGOs can often have more direct contact with poorer groups, thus ensuring that their help is geared directly to local needs.

(k) Many problems are very complicated. NGOs are finding it increasingly difficult to respond effectively to problems such as hunger, which often involve multinational institutions, such as the UN, and powerful interest groups and states.

*"It is not your right, it is your privilege to work with us. We don't want your charity, we want your co-operation."*
Woman in West Bengal, India, to Oxfam

# The International Red Cross and Red Crescent Movement

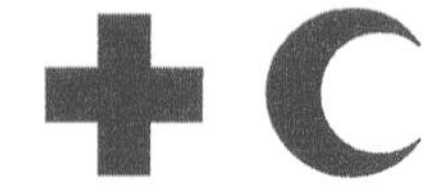

**The world's largest independent humanitarian network is a truly global community group.**

## Background

The International Red Cross and Red Crescent Movement began over 135 years ago. It was founded by Henry Dunant, a Swiss businessman, as a result of the appalling suffering of thousands of men, on both sides, who were left to die due to a lack of care after the Battle of Solferino in 1859. He proposed the creation of national relief societies, made up of volunteers, who were to be trained in peacetime to provide **neutral** and impartial help to relieve the suffering in times of war. In response to these ideas a committee, which later became the International Committee of the Red Cross, was set up in Geneva.

Henry Dunant also proposed that countries should adopt an international agreement, which would recognise the neutral status of medical services and of the wounded on the battlefield. This agreement, the original Geneva Convention, was adopted in 1864.

## The structure of the movement

There are three parts to this international movement:

### The International Committee of the Red Cross (ICRC)

The ICRC was created in 1863 and is the founding body of the movement. It is neutral and independent and therefore can work worldwide as an **intermediary** between both sides in a conflict. It also cares for the wounded, visits prisoners of war, restores contact between separated families, protects the civilian population and provides food or other assistance to conflict victims. It has an important role promoting and monitoring the application of international humanitarian law.

### International Federation of Red Cross and Red Crescent Societies

The International Federation was founded in 1919. Its tasks include:

- to encourage international assistance from national Red Cross and Red Crescent societies to disaster victims
- to encourage and promote the establishment and development of national societies
- to act as a permanent body of **liaison**, coordination and study for national societies

### National Red Cross and Red Crescent societies

There are over 175 recognised national Red Cross and Red Crescent societies around the world. National societies act as additional support to the public authorities in their own countries and provide a range of humanitarian services from disaster relief, health and social assistance to first-aid courses. During wartime, national societies support the army medical services. All national societies must first be recognised by the ICRC, in order to become part of the movement.

## The International Red Cross and Red Crescent Movement

The International Red Cross and the Red Crescent Movement is one of the largest humanitarian networks in the world. The Red Cross and Red Crescent are present in almost every country. All their activities have one central purpose:

'To prevent and **alleviate** human suffering wherever it may be found, to protect life and health and ensure respect for the human being, in particular in times of armed conflict and other emergencies, to work for the prevention of disease and for the promotion of health and social welfare, to encourage **voluntary service** and a constant readiness to give help by the members of the movement, and a universal sense of **solidarity** towards all those in need of its protection and assistance and thus contribute to the maintenance and promotion of peace.'

The movement has seven fundamental principles:

Humanity – To bring assistance to all who need it. To promote mutual understanding, friendship, cooperation and lasting peace amongst all peoples.

Impartiality – To make no discrimination as to nationality, race, religious beliefs, class or political opinions. To try to relieve the suffering of individuals, taking account only of their needs, and to give priority to the most urgent cases of distress.

Neutrality – In order to continue to enjoy the confidence of all, the movement may not take sides in hostilities or engage at any time in controversies of a political, racial or religious nature.

Independence – The movement is independent. National societies support the humanitarian services of their governments and follow its laws. But they must always remain separate from government, so that they can always act in accordance with the principles of the movement.

Voluntary service – It is a voluntary relief movement and does not produce any profit.

Unity – There can only be one Red Cross or one Red Crescent society in any one country. It must be open to all. It must carry on its humanitarian work throughout the whole of the country.

Universality – The International Red Cross and Red Crescent Movement, in which all societies have equal status and share equal responsibilities and duties in helping each other, is worldwide.

### TASKS

1. Imagine you are Henry Dunant. What inspired him to create the Red Cross/Red Crescent movement and what arguments do you think he may used to convince people to support him?.
2. Why would governments find it impossible to do what the Red Cross movement does?
3. Does being a voluntary organisation help the Red Cross and Red Crescent movement?
4. Design a recruitment poster highlighting the 'fundamental principles' of the movement, and encouraging people to volunteer as members.
5. What other organisations do you know about that share one or more of these principles? Choose one and research how it fulfils that principle. You could create a class presentation about different NGOs.

# Are emblems important?

**Over the years, millions of victims of war or natural disasters, the wounded, prisoners and refugees have seen the Red Cross and Red Crescent emblems as symbols of protection against the violence of warfare or the difficulties of disasters. For many the emblems represent the promise of a helping hand in a time of general distress and hope for peace.**

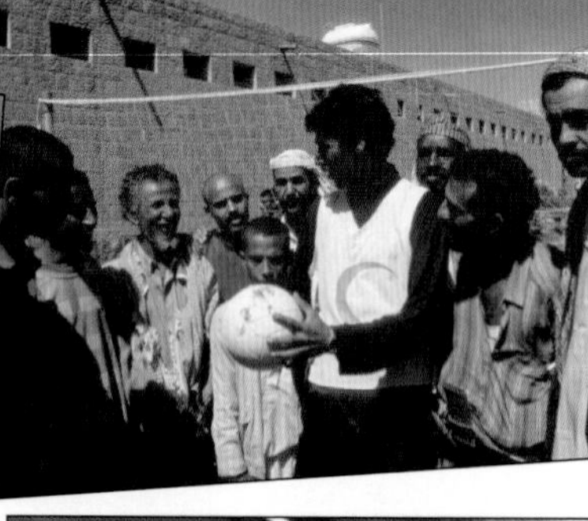

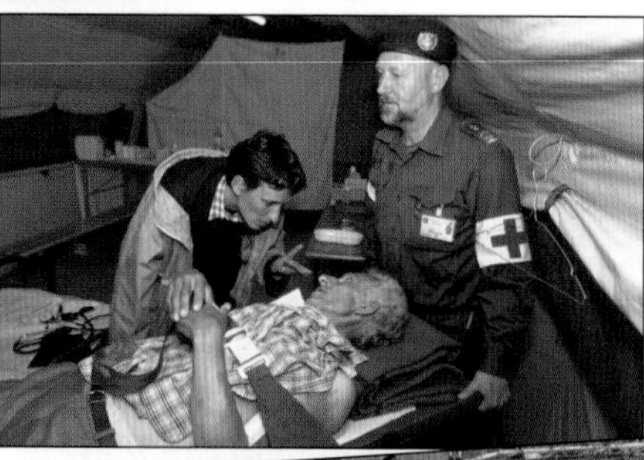

## TASK

1. Look at the photos taken throughout the world illustrating the different uses of the emblem. Match the following descriptions to the correct photos:

   Hospital ship

   Street theatre promoting the rules of war

   Transporting food

   A field hospital

   Armed forces medical vehicle

   Army exercises

   Bringing relief to earthquake victims

   Medical centre

   Volunteer with prisoners

   Field kitchen.

2. Use these images to start a list of all the practical things the movement does to meet its aims.
3. Carry out some further research to complete the list.

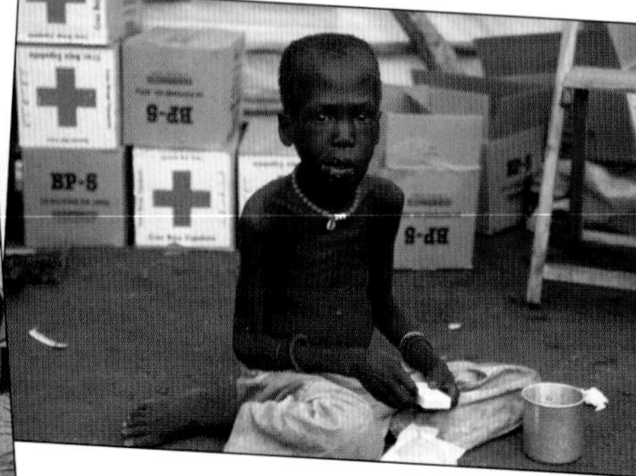

The symbols on the opposite page serve both as protection for military and civilian medical services in wartime and as distinctive signs for the national Red Cross and Red Crescent societies. But they have also been a source of difficulties. There have been many discussions and much has been written about the religious significance, or lack of it, in the Red Cross or Red Crescent emblems.

When Henry Dunant founded the movement, the adoption of one emblem to be common to everyone was important because in the nineteenth century each army used a different colour to mark its medical services. This made it impossible to identify members of the medical corps from fighting soldiers. The first international conference in 1863 did not select the symbol of a cross because it represented Christianity, it chose the red cross on a white flag because it was distinctive and easily recognisable.

## The creation of the Red Crescent

At the start of the Russo-Turkish war (1876–8) the Ottoman Empire, which had signed the Geneva Convention of 1864, declared that it would use a red crescent to mark its own ambulances because the distinctive sign of the red cross 'gave offence to Muslim soldiers', but they promised to respect the red cross sign protecting enemy ambulances. In 1929 a conference accepted the red crescent emblem but made a point of clearly stating that no new emblems would be recognised.

### Why change the emblem?

After the Second World War, at the 1949 International Conference, Israel proposed that a new emblem should be recognised, the red shield of David, which was used by the Israeli medical services. Some people believe that the emblems of the Red Cross and the Red Crescent cannot represent all nations equally because they appear to represent Christian and Muslim countries over those that follow other religions. They argue that a new single emblem with no national or religious links would be more appropriate.

## TASKS

1 Why do you think it is important to have a distinctive and recognisable symbol for the movement?

2 This is the latest proposal for an additional distinctive emblem. What do you think of the proposed emblem?

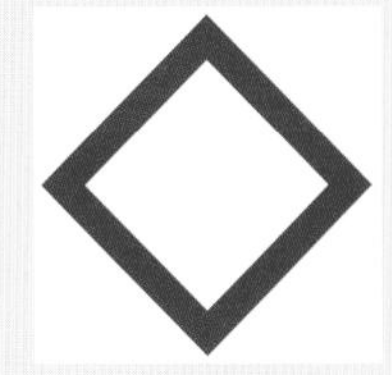

3 Can you come up with a better idea?

4 In your opinion do you think the current emblems should be changed?

In your answer include the following information:

Why were the two emblems originally adopted?

Arguments for changing the emblem

Arguments against

Conclusion (put forward your own solution if you think it would be better)

## EXTENSION TASK

1 Make a list of all the symbols and logos you know from international organisations and companies.

2 Draw some of the most effective logos and symbols from memory and compare them to others in the class.

3 Are you able to recall them accurately?

4 Do any of these logos represent something about their organisation? What?

5 What makes a good logo?

# Can conflicts be resolved peacefully?

**In this section you will begin to understand and question the causes of conflict, how peace can be brought about and how difficult it is to secure peace and reconciliation between opposing sides.**

> **SKILLS FOCUS**
> - Thinking about and understanding the causes of conflict
> - Justifying your opinion about practical solutions to conflict

## When will it ever end?

At the end of the Second World War in 1945, many believed that the war to end all wars had been fought and that the nations of the world would learn to live in peace and harmony. This has not been the case. Today there are more than 30 wars being fought around the world; since 1945 the world has never been at peace.

### TASKS

1. What point is the cartoonist making?
2. How many of the conflicts that were happening in 1985 are still unresolved today?
3. How many more can you add?

An argument between two people could easily grow into a dispute between two or more groups and perhaps even develop so that two or more countries end up in conflict with each other. Conflicts cannot be isolated. Local crises can escalate: for example, the Arab/Israeli, Kosovo/Serbia and Iraq/Kuwait conflicts have spilled over their national boundaries. They have become international conflicts.

> **USEFUL WORDS**
>
> **Conflict** – a fight or struggle
>
> **Reconciliation** – settling an argument or disagreement
>
> **Resolve** – solve a problem

### TASKS

1. Think of as many reasons as you can why conflicts take place. Copy the following spidergram and complete it by adding further reasons as to why these and other national and international conflicts take place.

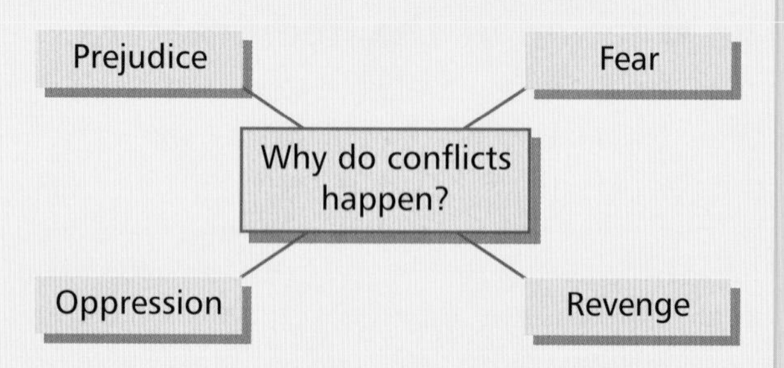


2. Think about which reasons are the more likely triggers for conflicts at a personal level, local/community level, nationally and globally, then copy and complete the table below.

| Level of conflict | Possible reasons for conflict | An example of an actual or possible conflict |
|---|---|---|
| Personal level | | |
| Local/community level | | |
| National level | | |
| Global level | | |

## The impact of conflicts

Whatever the reasons are behind a conflict, there are always winners and losers. More often than not the victims of conflicts are ordinary people and their environment.

### TASKS

What happens to communities as a result of wars? Team up with a partner to work on the following tasks.

1 Copy and complete the table at the foot of the page. Try and think of as many effects war can have as you can.

2 Look back at the work you have done on why conflicts take place. How could some of the conflicts you have listed be **resolved**? Give as many solutions as you can.

3 What is the more difficult, finding reasons for conflicts or the solutions? Why do you think this is so?

4 Who is responsible for resolving conflicts?

There are many organisations, groups and even individuals who try to bring about peace. They all have different roles to play but their aims are often the same. On the right is a list of the key players in international conflict resolution. Match them to the role in the activities column that best describes them.

| Key players in conflict resolution | Activities |
|---|---|
| (1) United Nations and its agencies | (a) They can provide direct support to individuals. They can often draw on members all around the world to help out with money, expertise or prayers. |
| (2) Governments/ superpowers such as the USA or the EU | (b) Provides negotiators and an international peace-keeping force. Soldiers are selected from countries which are not involved in the conflict. |
| (3) Non-Governmental Organisations – for example, Amnesty International | (c) Monitor the situation and publicise the information. They often encourage individuals across the world to put pressure on governments to stop human-rights violations. |
| (4) Religious groups | (d) Encourage both sides in a conflict to talk. They can also put pressure on governments by stopping trade with them, send in troops or provide arms to help one side in a conflict. |
| (5) Inspirational leaders like Nelson Mandela | (e) Help people see that there is a better way ahead by providing a role model. This is especially important to encourage people to show the forgiveness which is often important in creating peace and moving forward. |

| The effects of war on: | | | |
|---|---|---|---|
| **Adults** | **Children** | **Homes/local area** | **The country as a whole** |
| | | | |
| | | | |
| | | | |

# Peace and reconciliation – why is it so difficult to resolve conflicts?

## Focus on Sierra Leone

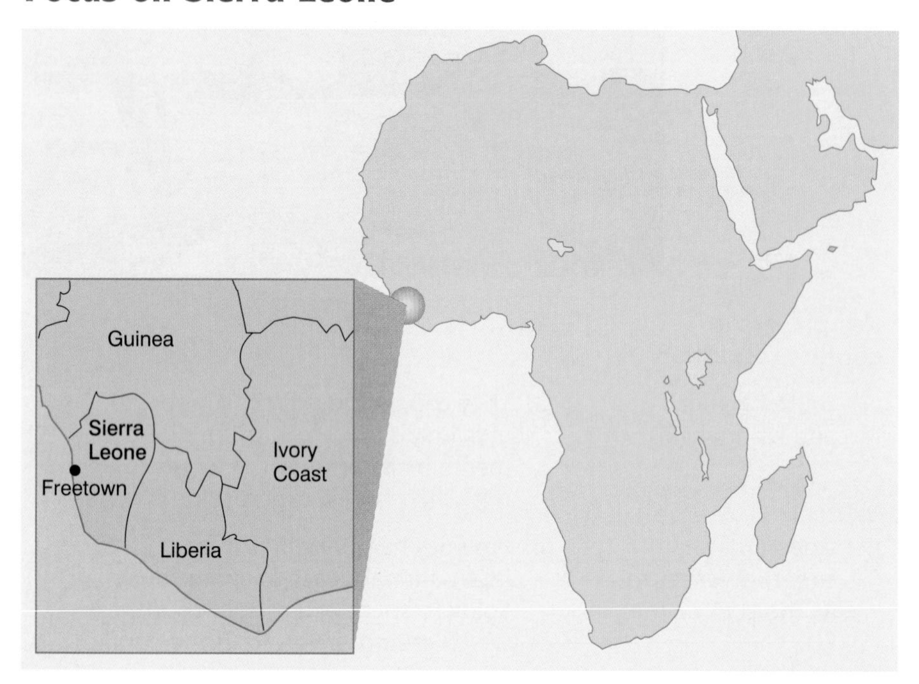


**USEFUL WORDS**

**Military coup** – a violent or illegal seizure of power by the army

**Depose** – remove a person or group from power

**Sanctions** – a punishment for breaking international law: for example, restricting trade

**Displaced** – a person forced to leave his/her own country because of war, fear, etc

**Infrastructure** – the basic foundations of the country, including roads, bridges, sewers and communication systems

**Disarmament** – to reduce weapons and military forces

**Amnesty** – a general pardon, to forgive a person or group for political offences

**Truth and reconciliation commission (TRC)** – a public hearing in which people involved in conflict come forward to admit what they did and ask for forgiveness

### What is this war about?

Sierra Leone gained independence from British rule in 1961 and since then there have been elected governments who have been in power for only a very short time. People accuse these governments of corruption. The vast majority of Sierra Leoneans have remained poor while a powerful elite ruled from the capital, Freetown. The rural poor grew increasingly resentful so that when the rebel movement, the Revolutionary United Front (RUF), was created there was no shortage of recruits.

There has been a civil war in Sierra Leone since 1991. The two main groups which are in conflict with each other are the national government and the RUF.

The RUF, led by Foday Sankoh (who was trained by the British army), wanted to get rid of corruption. They 'searched' for it everywhere. The RUF often attacked villagers they suspected of being government sympathisers. Outsiders were considered to be spies and many were kidnapped, including Africans from other countries and Europeans.

**TASKS**

1. Why do you think it was easy for the RUF to find volunteers for their rebel force?
2. Do you think there is democracy in Sierra Leone?
3. How could people let their government know if they are unhappy?
4. List all the problems you can find on these pages which contribute to the conflict in Sierra Leone.
5. Which problems are the most likely to prevent peace?
6. What role do international organisations hold?

### A summary of events

|  |  |
|---|---|
| April 1961 | Independence from British rule |
| 1991 | The RUF is formed |
| April 1992 | Captain Strasser, aged 26, ousts President Joseph Momoh in a **military coup** |
| February 1996 | Elections result in victory for Ahmed Tejan Kabbah's Sierra Leone People's Party |
| May 1997 | Major-General Johnny Paul Koroma **deposes** President Kabbah in a military coup, suspends the constitution, bans demonstrations and abolishes political parties. Kabbah flees to Guinea to raise international support |
| July 1997 | The Commonwealth suspends Sierra Leone |
| October 1997 | The UN imposes **sanctions** against Sierra Leone |
| February 1998 | The Nigerian-led West African intervention force , ECOMOG, storms the capital, Freetown |
| March 1998 | President Kabbah makes a triumphant return |
| January 1999 | RUF rebels, led by Foday Sankoh, seize parts of Freetown from ECOMOG. After weeks of fighting the rebels are driven out |
| May 1999 | A ceasefire is agreed. In hospitals and amputee camps, victims of rebel atrocities express the hope that eight years of civil war may soon be over |
| July 1999 | Six weeks of talks in the Togolese capital, Lome, result in a peace agreement, under which rebels receive posts in government and assurances that they will not be prosecuted for war crimes |
| November 1999 | UN troops arrive to police the peace agreement but one rebel leader, Sam Bokari, says they are not welcome. Meanwhile ECOMOG troops are attacked outside Freetown |
| April 2000 | UN forces come under attack in the east, 50 troops are abducted |
| May 2000 | Rebel leader Foday Sankoh is captured, Britain announces a military-assistance plan for the government, and the UN soldiers are released |
| July 2000 | British military force sent to help restore order leaves |
| August 2000 | The UN agrees to pursue rebels through an international tribunal |

**The effects of the conflict**
The civil war has **displaced** half the country's 4.5 million population. At least 50,000 people have died in the fighting and there are an estimated 100,000 victims of mutilation. The economy is in ruins and the country's **infrastructure** has collapsed.

## Peace deals: will they or won't they work?

In November 1996, the Sierra Leonean government and the RUF had a peace agreement called the Abidjon Accord. It failed because the army and RUF took control of the government in May 1997. President Kabbah escaped to neighbouring Guinea.

In October 1997, the army and RUF, now ruling the country, signed a peace plan with the exiled President Kabbah. This initiative failed because the plan was never put into action.

In July 1999, President Kabbah, the democratically elected leader of the country, and the rebel RUF forces agreed a peace deal, the Lome Peace Accord. Under the agreement, leaders of the RUF were to be allowed to become government ministers. Human-rights organisations criticised the inclusion of the RUF in government, saying the rebels had used killings, rapes and mutilations to gain a place at the negotiating table after nine years of war. The UN was given the job of overseeing RUF **disarmament**, but thousands of rebel gunmen remained at large, and the RUF still controlled much of the country.

## Forgiving the unforgivable

Many people believe that peace deals have not worked because people at the grassroots did not know about them. The following extracts are examples of how Sierra Leone and its people are trying to make peace work.

### (A) Peace On-Air

Journalist Andrew Kromah risks his life to broadcast unbiased news to Sierra Leone's rural communities. He explains the key role of Radio Bo in the country's fragile peace process.

'I established Radio Bo in the firm belief that impartial, vigorous and diverse broadcasting is the key to an active civil society movement for peace and development in an emerging democracy.'

Radio Bo was established in 1993. It is an independent station broadcasting to a population of over 2.5 million inhabitants.

'At Radio Bo we believe a major obstacle to the peace process is a lack of communication between parties to the conflict and insufficient information disseminated to citizens. ... Sierra Leoneans expressed fear of the rebels and disgust with the **amnesty**, which was part of the 1999 Lome Peace Accord – they accepted it in their eagerness for peace. When President Kabbah toured the country, urging people to forgive and forget, people questioned whether this was possible without justice.'

Philip John Bull, President of the Amputees Association, said on a recent phone-in programme, 'Some of us want to forgive, but the Government is not helping us. Instead they are caring for those who amputated us. We feel bad about that and now they are asking us to reconcile. The rebels ... must be tried for justice'.

Sierra Leoneans welcome the proposed UN-authorised war-crimes tribunal: they see this court as the only way to make rebel fighters see reason and lay down their arms. Fatmata Sannoh, a fishmonger, lost her husband and three children in the war, she says, '(rebel leaders like) Foday Sankoh and other rebels must be tried for crimes against humanity and then be sentenced to life imprisonment'.

From *Orbit*, the magazine of the VSO, Autumn 2000)

### (B) Moment of Truth

'I will forgive, but I will not forget. Whenever I walk or look at myself in a mirror I always remember 11 January 1999,' says Kiadiatu Fofanah. Five days earlier, rebels of the RUF had invaded the capital, Freetown. They attacked Fofanah and her family, hacking off her legs and killing her two nephews. 'After amputating my legs I was left to die on the hillside of Kissy, in the east of Freetown,' she says. It was three days before she was discovered. It is a miracle she survived; Fofanah is still haunted by the horror of her ordeal. With her nine children she lives in a camp for amputees in Freetown. 'With all this in mind, how can I be reconciled with these rebels who do not show any sign of remorse for their wrong doing?'

From *Orbit*, Autumn 2000)

### Thinking about conflict resolution

Countries that have suffered from civil wars and other types of violent conflict find it difficult to move ahead and build peace. There are often too many bad memories and painful losses to just forget what has happened; but if people spend too much time thinking about how terrible the past was, it makes it difficult to go forward and face the future.

Hold a class discussion to decide on ways to resolve conflicts. You could start with the case of Sierra Leone, but think about the general issues you would have to consider as well. Governments have to think about:

- justice for those who suffered
- fairness to everyone
- a solution that is practical
- a balance between everyone's interests.

### (C) Forum of Conscience

Many Sierra Leoneans and human-rights activists were not happy with the Lome Peace Accord, which gave amnesty to rebels, so when the agreement collapsed, a coalition of more than 40 community and human-rights organisations stepped up their campaign for a credible **truth and reconciliation commission** (TRC). Opinion polls indicated strong support among Sierra Leoneans for rebel leaders to stand trial. While the UN-authorised war-crimes court is welcome, there is still a need for a truth commission. Tamba Brima, a farmer who lost his wife and children in the conflict, explains why:

'Let the leadership of the different fighting factions face justice because they are the architect of our suffering; the foot soldiers and children can go through the TRC because these people were misled by their leaders,' he says.

Not everyone agrees on the need for either a commission or a court. 'These will open up old wounds,' says Mohamed Sesay, a former rebel soldier. 'Let us forget and forgive one another, as we are all Sierra Leonean,' he says. 'But without a commission, reconciliation will be impossible,' argues Pa Ngauja, a schoolteacher who lost his family and had his hands amputated during a rebel attack. 'To eliminate the deep-seated bitterness, the scale of atrocities must be understood; those who perpetrated untold crimes should own up to their deeds and show some remorse; only then can we have lasting reconciliation,' he says. For Fofanah, the credibility of the commission will depend on the government's ability to deliver basic needs to people who can no longer fend for themselves. But she says, 'In the interest of lasting peace in the country, I accept the commission and hope it will be a credible and independent process.'

From a report by John Caulker of the human-rights organisation, Forum of Conscience

Three possible solutions to conflict are given below:

1 **Justice**
In Serbia the wartime leader, Slobodan Milosevic, was prosecuted by the new government and was also pursued by the International War Crimes Tribunal.

2 **Finding the Truth**
In South Africa, people who had plotted and harmed others were not prosecuted for their crimes if they attended the Truth and Reconciliation Committee, established to uncover the whole truth about what happened under apartheid.

3 **Ignoring the Problem**
In Chile, for many years General Pinochet and his supporters, some of whom were thought to have been responsible for many murders, were allowed to retire without facing any action or charges.

## TASKS

**1** List the different ways in which people have tried to find peace in Sierra Leone.

**2** Why do you think many of the peace deals that were agreed upon have failed? What other reasons can you think of for peace deals failing in conflict situations?

Try to think about the following questions both from your own point of view and that of someone like Kiadiatu Fofanah (in source B):

**3** How does the amnesty given to the rebels in the Lome Peace Accord make you feel?

**4** Why do you think Mohamed Sesay (source C) believes that there is no need for a commission or court?

**5** How would you go about bringing peace to Sierra Leone? Do you think the policy of forgiving and forgetting is the best way forward? Or do you think a truth and reconciliation commission is better? Give reasons for your opinions.

# The power of words and images

**Words and images matter. They have the power to shape the way we understand and relate to people and different ways of living. Images of conflicts and disasters, especially from developing countries, shown in news reports and charity advertisements, are often negative and over-simplified. They can have a lasting effect on the way we see other nations and communities. It is important to consider how and why these images are chosen and the impact they have on us.**

*"In general the third world doesn't have much coverage, we tend to cover it with a single hit … discover something terrible, cover it, leave it."*

Michael Burke, TV news presenter

*"You go where there is trouble; you go where there is a disaster; you go to report on these disasters. Disasters, trouble, fighting, bloodshed, killings. They make good television pictures."*

Trevor McDonald, TV news presenter

## USEFUL WORDS

**Developing countries** – countries that are poor and are trying to develop their economies

## SKILLS FOCUS

- Interpret different forms of media
- Understand how the media affects opinions

## TASK

1 Think of any country you consider to be a **developing country**, then copy and complete the questions on the star diagram below. Start at the top and work clockwise. Follow up with some research to find out how accurate your ideas were.

2 Study news coverage or other media images of developing countries or collect advertisements from charities who work in developing countries. Do the images share anything in common?

3 Why do you think some images are chosen over others?

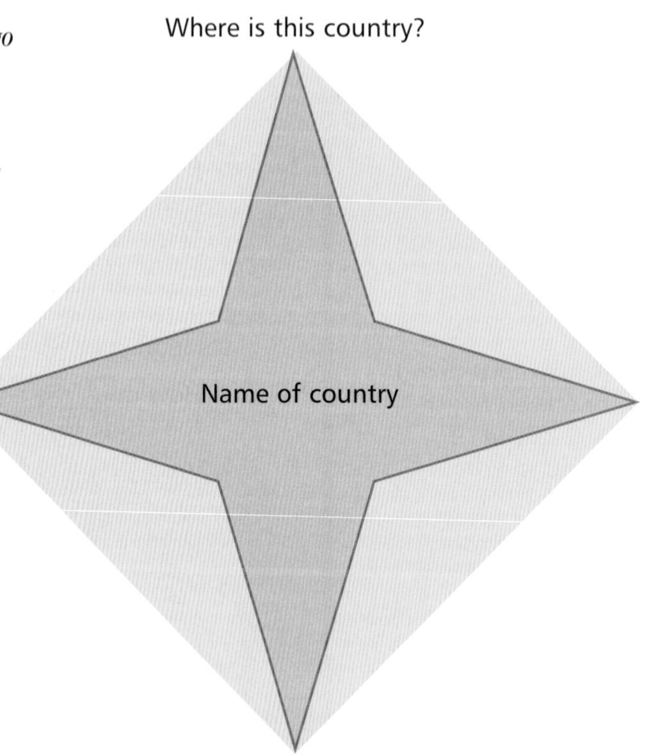

# FREED AFTER 56 HOURS BUT 20,000 FEARED DEAD

## INDIAN EARTHQUAKE DISASTER

SMOKE from **funeral pyres** mixes with the stench of **decomposing** bodies and the sickly sweet scent of lime and chlorine.

Exhausted rescuers, caked in dust and sweat and armed with every tool at hand – including screwdrivers and spanners – gouge at the rubble.

Their efforts are rewarded when they finally pull out a woman who has been pinned beneath a ceiling fan and rubble for 56 hours.

Amazingly, Kusam D Soni, who is in her mid-thirties, emerges with a huge smile and walks over to her waiting husband.

Meanwhile, other rescuers wielding a metal pole punch at the mangled concrete and metal girders, pausing to listen for a baby's cry.

The troops move from flattened building to flattened building, listening for signs of life.

Sometimes they use pneumatic rams, more often hammers and screwdrivers, scraping at this city of 200,000 people which has become a vision of hell.

Rescuers from around the world last night offered the last glimmer of hope for the victims of India's devastating earthquake.

Ashok, 40, a father of two and a consultant community paediatrician in Fareham, Gosport, Hants, had travelled to India to scatter his late mother's ashes in the River Ganges and to attend a one-day medical conference in Agra. He was killed when a building collapsed.

Yesterday his wife, Chaya, flew out to the scene of the tragedy. As the death toll climbed towards 20,000, dazed survivors searched for whatever food they could find from wrecked shops.

Thousands remained buried under tonnes of rubble.

At Ahmedabad, where 50 multi-storey buildings collapsed, the city hospital is already overflowing, bandaged patients lie outside hooked up to intravenous drips hanging from bushes.

The bodies of those who could not be helped lined the corridors.

The earthquake, measuring 7.9 on the Richter Scale, was felt up to 1,200 miles from the epicentre.

Last night the emphasis began to shift from the dead to the survivors. With no water or electricity supplies officials fear an epidemic of disease.

Neighbouring Pakistan, where the quake killed at least 15 people, puts aside its differences with nuclear rival India, and said it would help the global relief effort.

### GLOSSARY

**Funeral pyres** – bonfires on which corpses are burnt

**Decomposing** – rotting

**Paediatrician** – doctor who specialises in the treatment of children

### TASKS

1. Look at the 'Freed after 56 hours' extract on the Indian earthquake. Without looking at the individual paragraphs, how do the main headline and the photograph make you feel?
2. Now look at the whole article. Write down the words or phrases that affect how you feel.
3. Why do you think certain kinds of words and images are chosen in accounts about developing countries?
   (a) Write the reasons at the foot of the page out onto individual cards, then add as many other reasons you can think of to make up a set of cards.
   (b) Put the cards in order of importance and discuss them with others.

To grab people's attention

To make people sorry for others

To persuade people to give money

# Analysing the media

**There are many different ways of presenting the same news story. The paragraphs on the previous page were taken from an article in one type of British newspaper. Below is a selection of articles from a range of newspapers and other published sources covering the same news story.**

## TASKS

1. Compare the news stories and then copy and complete the table using evidence from the articles. Alternatively, you could use a selection of sources you have collected yourself on a story that interests you.
2. Were there major differences in how the news story was reported in the different types of media?
3. Were you surprised by your findings? If so, why?
4. How has this exercise affected your understanding of the media?

| Source | Type of media source, e.g. newspaper | Headline | How does the article make me feel? | Is anybody quoted? Where are they from? | Whose point of view is the story told from? | What impression of the country does the article give? |
|---|---|---|---|---|---|---|
| | | | | | | |
| | | | | | | |
| | | | | | | |

▼ **Article A**

**Environment News Service**

# Death Tolls Climb in India's Worst Earthquake

Ahmedabad, India, January 29, 2001 – at least 25,000 people have died and many thousands more are critically injured and missing as a result of an earthquake measuring 7.9 on the Richter Scale that shook western India on Friday, India's 52nd Republic Day.

The government of India has decided that while there will be no appeal for assistance, all offers made voluntarily will be gratefully accepted. India has received offers of assistance from a large number of foreign countries and aid agencies.

Search and rescue help is welcome including sniffer dogs, electronic equipment for searching for bodies and cutting concrete slabs, communication equipment, as well as mobile surgical-operation theatres and other medical hardware.

Offers for supply of clothes and tents will be accepted if they can be airlifted to Ahmedabad. Medical and rescue teams will be welcomed provided they come in their own aircraft.

Government control rooms are functioning round the clock. All Indian Armed Forces and Security Forces are employed in rescue operations and other relief activities.

The central government and several state governments have sent additional medical teams together with medicine and medical equipment and supplies. The Indian Ministry of Health is sending a special team to check outbreak of epidemics.

▼ Article B

**International Herald Tribune**

# DESOLATION AT EPICENTER

Celia W Dugger, *New York Times* Service — Monday, January 29, 2001

## Quake Toll May Hit 20,000 India Aide says

**BHUJ, India.** Here, near the epicenter of the wrathful earthquake that shook the Subcontinent, thousands are dead and hundreds of thousands are sleeping under starry skies in the chilly winter air, warmed by small campfires that flicker, wherever there is open ground.

One family of five sat Sunday, as they have since the earthquake, on thin cloths laid out in front of a Hindu temple. Kusum Naresh Soni, mother of three, was still in the apricot-coloured nightgown she was wearing when she ran out of her crumbling home.

She said her family had no blankets to keep them warm and only the clothes on their backs. Her husband's jewellery shop also collapsed, burying his inventory of gold and destroying his livelihood.

'We're sitting here praying to God,' she said. 'We don't know what to do.'

Despite the hardships, Mrs Thakkar and many others interviewed on Sunday seem more plucky than downcast. Even the cold night and hard ground elicited mainly philosophical shrugs. They said they were grateful to be alive and determined to rebuild.

'I can work as a maid or take in laundry or cook food,' Mrs Thakkar said. 'Somehow we will survive.'

▼ Article C

**Oxfam**

# EARTHQUAKE IN INDIA

At least 10,000 people are reported dead after a series of strong earthquakes measuring between 6.9 and 7.9 on the Richter scale, hit the northwest Indian state of Gujarat on Friday morning (26 January).

Oxfam has strong links with the Gujarat state authorities as a result of its drought-response programme, which started in May 2000.

Despite the difficulty in obtaining up-to-the minute information, Oxfam Field Programme Manager, John Samual, reported from Ahmedabad early on Friday afternoon that it has not yet been possible to reach affected rural areas. Oxfam has put together a team of experts to fly out to Gujarat early next week to join local staff, who are already assessing how Oxfam can best help.

▼ Article D

*Times of India*

# Indian-origin expert leads Swiss rescue team

**AHMEDABAD: When Swiss rescue worker Karvin Ahuja came vacationing to Goa earlier this year, little did he know he would soon be returning to India in an official capacity as a rescue worker in the earthquake-ravaged Gujarat.**

'I've been to India several times and I was in Goa and Chennai three weeks ago for a holiday but I never thought I would have to return under these circumstances,' said the 29-year-old Ahuja.

Clad in bright orange overalls and aided by nine specially trained sniffer dogs, the men and women of the 48-strong Swiss team have fanned out all over the city, working with state police in rescue operations.

'Some members of our team have already moved out to Bhuj and we will join them here as soon as we can,' said the six-feet-tall Ahuja, who was a member of Swiss teams that participated in relief operations in earthquake-affected areas of Turkey and Taiwan in 1999.

Expressing surprise at the fact that some buildings here had collapsed while others remained almost unharmed by the tremors, Ahuja said, 'One would assume there was something wrong with the construction of the buildings that collapsed. We encountered something similar in the quake-affected areas of Turkey (as in Gujarat), the ground was dry and hard but the buildings that collapsed were high rise structures that were not properly constructed.'

'In Taiwan, however, the ground was soggy but the buildings were well-made. They just sank into the ground,' he said.

# Questioning photographs

**Do images always give you the complete picture? Have you ever thought about why and how certain images are used? Photographs can have a powerful influence on our beliefs and opinions about places and/or stories. But a photograph does not always give you the whole story.**

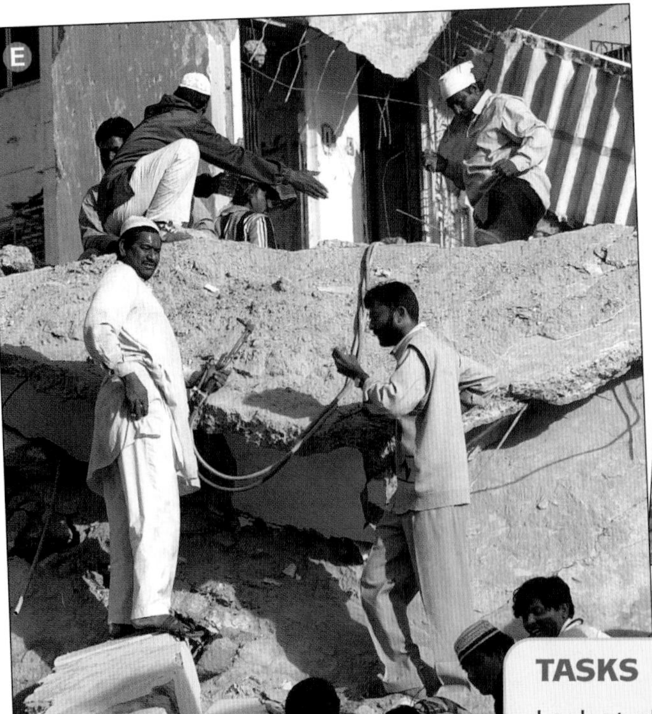
E

F

G

## TASKS

Look at photographs A to G, which show the effects of the devastating earthquake that took place on 26 January 2001 in India.

Now look at photograph A:

1 What is your first impression of the photograph?

2 How would you describe it, as being positive, negative or neutral?

3 Think of three captions for the photograph, one positive, one negative and one neutral.

4 Do the captions change your interpretation of the photograph?

Choose two photographs from B to E:

5 What impression do the photographs give?

6 Would the photographs be suitable for a family newspaper?

7 What do you think is happening outside the frame of the photograph?

8 What caption would you give each photograph?

How do you like to be photographed?

9 Think of three situations where you would be happy to have your photograph taken.

10 Think of three situations where you would not like your photograph taken.

Explain why you have chosen these particular situations.

Now look at photographs F and G:

11 Would you have liked to have been photographed in this situation? Give reasons for your answers.

12 Would you have allowed yourself to be photographed?

13 Should the subject of the photograph have any rights over how their photograph is to be used?

# Making a difference to debt

**The world cannot be viewed just as a collection of separate countries. It is also a system of interacting parts with a range of links, but these links are not always equal. You not only need to be aware of your connections with other parts of the world, but you also need to question where the links came from, how they operate and whose interest they serve. Understanding these issues will help you to become informed and active citizens of the global community in which you live.**

*"Never doubt that a group of thoughtful, committed citizens can change the world. Indeed it's the only thing that ever has."*

Margaret Mead, anthropologist

**SKILLS FOCUS**

- Understanding debt as a global issue and thinking about local action

## Working for change

It can sometimes feel as if individuals are helpless to create change, that we do not have the power or the issues are just too complicated. But thousands of people working together can achieve change, even when facing global problems.

There are some common questions to think about when planning action:

(1) What is the problem?
(2) What causes the problem?
(3) What might affect the causes?
(4) What is the preferred outcome?
(5) Who could help?
(6) What should be done?

**USEFUL WORDS**

**Lobbying** – trying to get your point across to a decision-maker

**Endorsement** – backing or supporting someone or something

**Independence** – the state a country is in when it rules itself

**Export** – goods sold abroad and leaving a country

**Import** – goods bought abroad and coming into a country

**G8** – the group of the eight most powerful countries in the world

**An Example of People Power – the Grameem Bank, Bangladesh**

The banking system generally deals with large amounts of money and businesses. Poor individual people have little chance of getting very small loans, especially if they have no property of their own to use as a guarantee for the bank. Professor Mohammed Yunus realised that a bank which lent very small amounts of money to poor people just to get them started in a business would help them make a huge difference to their lives. The example he quotes is of a woman who borrowed money from a bamboo merchant to buy the bamboo to make stools; when she sold the stools to the merchant he set the price so low that she only made 2 pence a day. When the Grameem bank started, it lent her the money to buy the bamboo herself so she could sell to anyone and make more money. Of the bank's customers, 94 per cent are women and 98 per cent of its loans are paid back. The bank now reaches over half of all the villages in Bangladesh, has been copied in dozens of other countries, and aims to reach one third of all the world's poor people by the year 2005. The bank aims to eliminate poverty rather than make profits.

# Case-study: the Jubilee 2000 campaign

**There is nothing like a major turning-point in time to focus energies and create hope. With the coming of the 21st century, the new millennium, there was a sense of optimism and energy, a belief that things could be changed to make the world a fairer place. One step towards this ideal was to call for the cancellation of the unpayable debt owed by the world's poorest countries. This global campaign came to be known as Jubilee 2000.**

## Why Jubilee 2000?

Campaigns to forgive the debts of the poorest nations are nothing new. So what was so special about this campaign? The difference was that it did not restrict itself to **lobbying** policymakers, but aimed its message at many levels of society. The campaign was taken on to the streets and into the mainstream media. It received the official **endorsement** of various churches and religious groups, from the Pope to Anglican bishops, from rabbis to imams (Muslim leaders). It had popular support and appeal.

Yoko Kitasawa, co-chair of the Jubilee 2000 Japan, considers the Jubilee campaign was 'the most successful campaign uniting trade unions, religious groups, NGOs and other social movements working for the impoverished people of Africa and the South'.

*"We want nothing less than to enter the new millennium as one world."*

Mulima Kufekisa Akapelwa, Zambian CAFOD partner, 1998

### TASKS

1. Where are most Heavily Indebted Poor Countries in the world?
2. What do you know about these countries?
3. What message is the cartoon trying to get across?

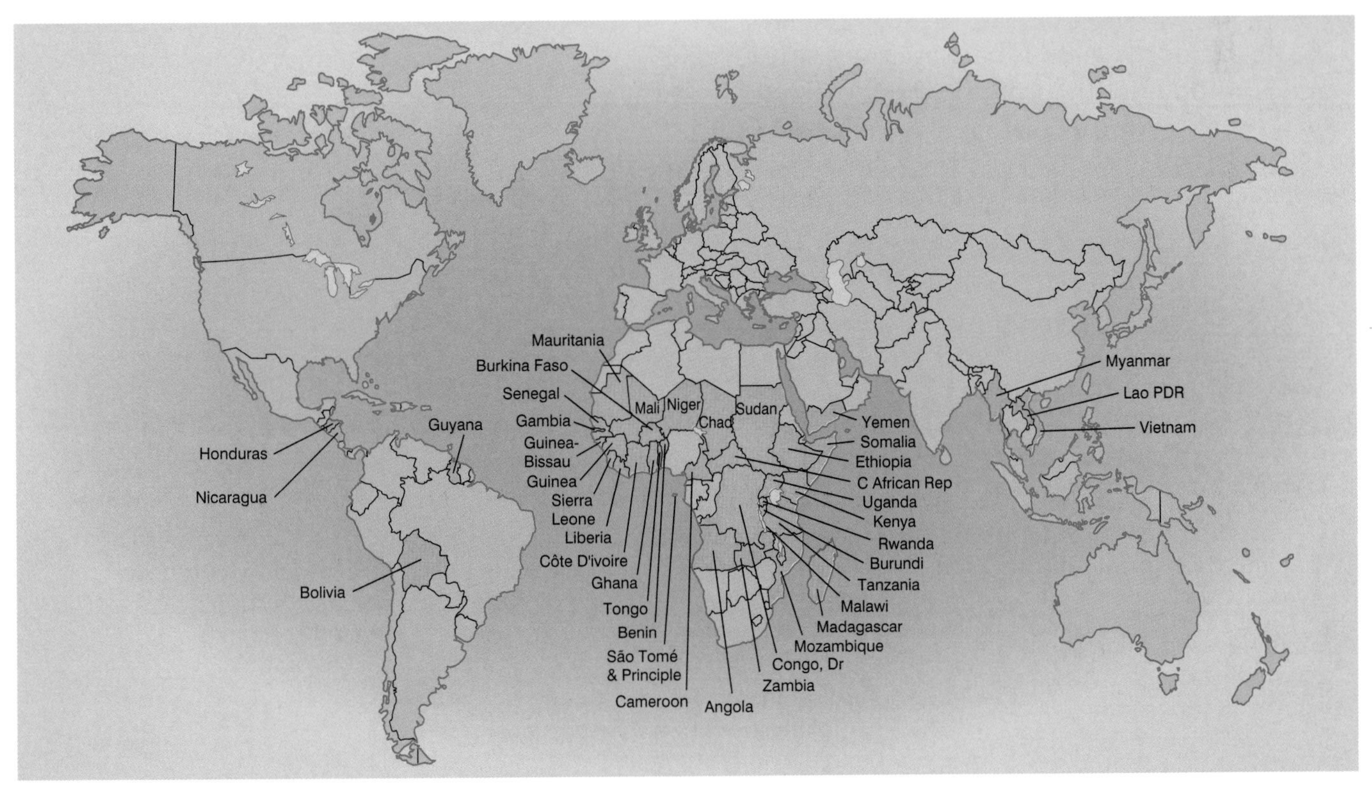


▲ **The debt map**

## The history of debt

# Out of Africa

*Navigator*, northerner, is looking down on Africa
studying the evidence as if it were a chart,
*pronouns* yet *possessive* as he measures every boundary,
apparently investing in a human hypermarket.

Gazing down the aisles he sees images of bargain buys,
casual *cartography* and rivers at his beck;
European architects and long-forgotten *demagogues*
whisper words of nonsense by the soft nape of his neck.

This was Belgian, Portuguese. Or *confiscated* property
whenever northern premises were under any threat;
power was the ruler's as it drew its straight and narrow line
for which of course all Africans are ever in our debt.

Northerners (or 'Westerners', for so they like to style themselves)
trampled on this continent like animals on mud.
They carved it up like surgeons and disposed of precious memories,
returning precious little but *coagulated* blood.

Navigator, northerner, is banking over Africa,
and counting up the profit on the old colonial crown,
flying over territory once his private *crucible*,
and always looking backwards when he isn't looking down.

Bill Greenwell, *New Statesman and Society*, 8 April 1994

**navigator** – someone who plots the course for a ship

**possessive pronouns** – eg mine, yours, theirs

**cartography** – map-making

**demagogue** – a person who tries to win power by appealing to people's emotions

**confiscated** – taken away, usually as a punishment

**coagulated** – thickened, clotted

**crucible** – melting pot; severe test or trial

## TASKS

1. Read the poem then write a character profile of the 'Navigator'
2. Why do you think the writer compares Africa to a giant supermarket?
3. Many of the words and phrases in the poem have a double meaning. Explain the two meanings of each of the following:
   - ruler
   - [Africans are] in our debt
   - looking down on Africa

   Can you find any more?
4. Choose one verse from the poem and write down what you think the poet is really trying to say.

## How the debt crisis happened

### The struggle for independence

After the Second World War there was a worldwide movement in the countries that had been ruled by the West to gain their **independence**. But as countries became independent and tried to develop their economies, another set of problems emerged – the debt crisis was one of these.

**Up to the 1960s**
Many poor, newly independent countries relied on exporting crops to generate the money they needed to buy manufactured goods from the West. They also relied on importing oil for their own economic needs.

**Early 1970s**
The oil-producing countries reduced their production of oil. Less oil available meant that the price went up. Overall the price rose by 400 per cent and the extra profits the oil-producing countries made were deposited in banks.

**During the 1970s**
Banks make money when they lend money to other people, who then pay interest on the loan. The banks had lots of money from the oil profits to invest, and the poor countries needed to borrow money to help them pay for the expensive oil and the Western-manufactured goods they wanted (these goods were more expensive because the oil prices had an effect on the manufacturers' costs).

**By the early 1980s**
Interest rates began to rise. This meant that the loans taken out by poor countries began to cost them more. At the same time, the prices of the crops sold by poor countries were falling. By 1987, a farmer had to sell 6 times the amount of cotton that he would have done in 1972, in order to buy a truck.

**1982**
Mexico threatened to stop paying interest completely. The banks panicked because if all countries were to have followed Mexico's example, all the money loaned out would never have been recovered. The IMF, which provides short-term loans to governments (see Chapter 5, Democracy), offered Mexico new loans to pay off its old ones and longer periods of repayment.

**Since the 1980s**
To stop countries failing to repay loans, new loans have been issued so that old loans can be repaid. This means the poor indebted countries can never break out of the cycle of debt built up by their governments nearly thirty years ago.

## TASKS

1. Is anyone to blame for the debt crisis?
   (a) Make a list of all the people and organisations involved.
   (b) Write a sentence about each.
   (c) Do you think that any other factors helped cause the problems?
2. How is an indebted country different from an indebted company?

## Resisting debt

The scale of the effects of the debt trap on the people in the developing world is huge. Initial resistance against the IMF and World Bank policies took the form of strikes and demonstrations. One of the bloodiest IMF riots took place in 1984, in the Dominican Republic, when the price of basic foodstuffs doubled and the price of medicines went up by 400 per cent. Four days of rioting left 112 people dead and 500 wounded. As debt has continued to increase, a more coordinated people's response has emerged. Groups have formed in the debtor countries to raise awareness of how debt is linked to many of the economic and social problems that people are facing.

### Action around the globe

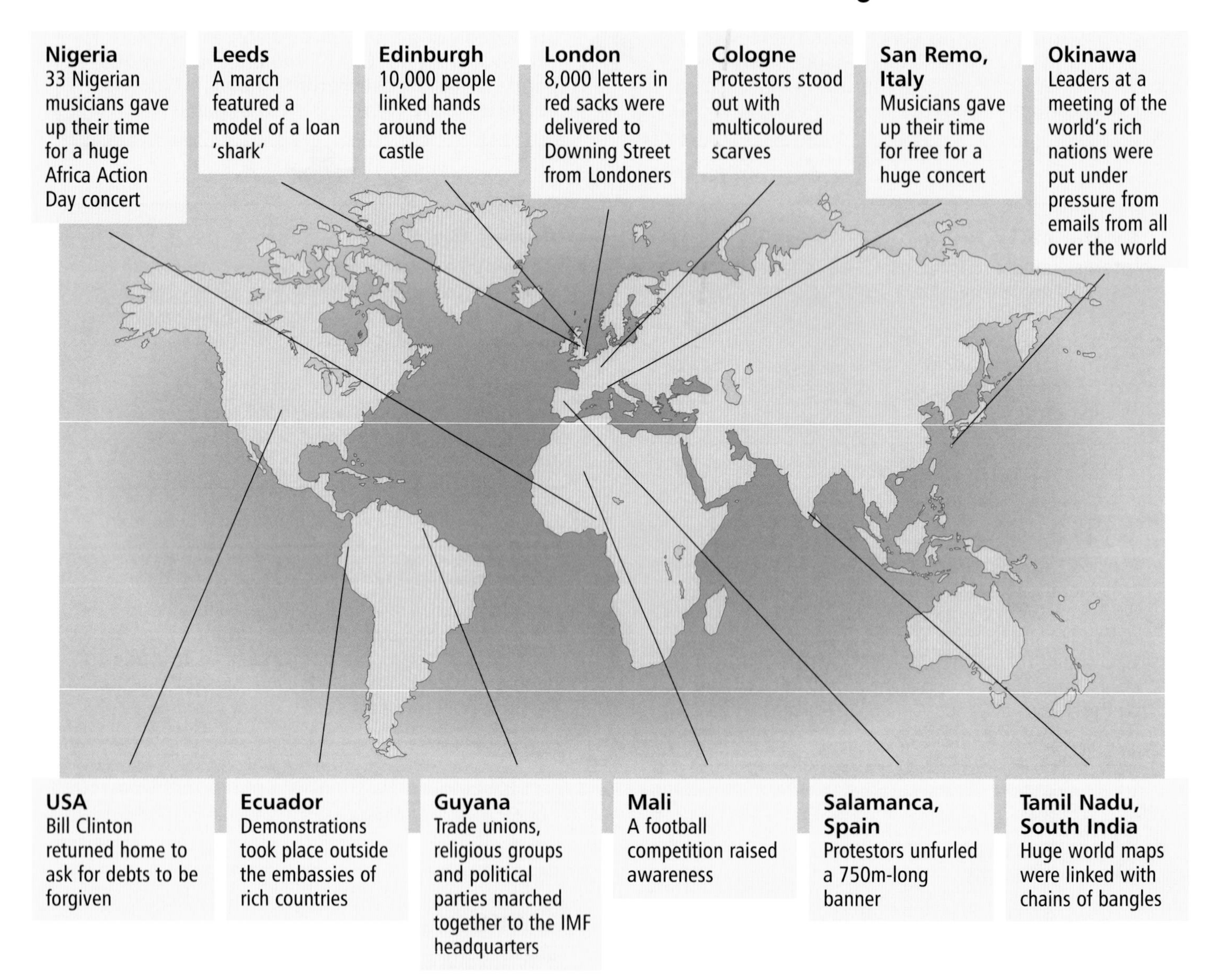


### How much debt has been cancelled so far?

A total of 22 countries were given some debt relief by the IMF, World Bank and Western governments. This is less than half the number of countries that Jubilee 2000 viewed as urgently requiring relief. On average, these countries will have their debt service payments reduced by one third. Other successes include the announcement by the British Government in December 2000 either to cancel outright or hold in trust all payments made by indebted countries to the UK. However, by the end of the year 2000, Jubilee 2000 thought that there was still a long way to go.

## What happens next?

By 31 December 2000, Jubilee 2000 had ended their campaign but their work was not finished. Three new projects were established:

- Drop the Debt
  A short-term campaign to lobby political leaders in the run-up to the **G8** Summit (a meeting of the world's richest countries) in Genoa, Italy, in July 2001. It officially closed down shortly after this meeting.
- Jubilee Plus
  A longer-term project that calls itself a 'Think and Do Tank'. It carries out research into the problem of international debt, lobbies decision-makers, publishes information and helps to maintain international links between debt campaigners.
- The Jubilee Debt Campaign
  This UK organisation continues the work of the Jubilee 2000 campaign. It has individual and organisational membership from all over the country.

### Action

The Drop the Debt campaign is only one example where people have joined together to bring about change. There are many ways in which individuals can make their voice heard either alone or by working in groups.

How many different examples of individual and group action can you think of?

### TASKS

Copy and complete the table below.

1 Look at the list below and choose which actions can be done by individuals and which in groups (some actions may be carried out by both).

2 Add in examples of other actions, either from this chapter or from your own experience.

3 Can you think of any examples where the action has been successful in challenging decision-makers or bringing about change?

4 Design a new media campaign for one of the three projects that have replaced Jubilee 2000. What can you say to keep people interested?

| Action taken | Individual | Group | Example of when used |
|---|---|---|---|
| Boycott companies that produce environmentally harmful products | | | |
| Sign a petition | | | |
| Write a letter to your MP or leader of another country | | | |
| Set up a campaigning group in school or in the local community | | | |
| Learn some facts about an issue and mention them in conversation, spread the message by word and mouth | | | |
| Perform a drama highlighting what you are campaigning for | | | |
| Boycott products that come from countries where human rights are violated | | | |
| Use the media to highlight what is happening | | | |
| Boycott products from companies that exploit the workforce | | | |

*Some people argue that cancelling debt is too simplistic. They say allowing governments to keep more money does not necessarily help the poorest people in those countries.*

*What do you think?*

# Writing your project

The Internet is a useful place to find information about global issues. Not only does it provide a way for people to publicise what they are doing but it can also be an effective tool for linking people and encouraging action across the world.

The following websites are helpful starting points for research into the issues covered in this book:

## One World Net
**www.oneworld.org**

An information and resource site covering a range of topical issues including human rights, globalisation and sustainable development. The site offers special reports, multimedia and news as well as information about individual countries

## Save The Children
**www.savethechildren.org**

An international charity, active in over 70 countries. The site is full of information about a wide range of issues relating to children including child labour, refugees and rights. It also has links to other NGOs

## Oxfam International
**www.oxfam.org**

Oxfam is an international organisation working with many different partners around the world to fight poverty and injustice. The website includes a wealth of information on a wide range of issues from fair trade to land reform to debt. It also has excellent links to other NGOs including Action Aid, Drop the Debt and UNICEF

## Europa
**www.citizens.eu.int**

The information service for the European Commission – the site includes the history of the EU, policies, background information on European institutions, the day's main European news and reports on the activities of the European Parliament

## UN
**www.un.org**

Everything you need to know about the UN – publications, databases, reports and documents on all aspects of its work from human rights to economic and social development

## Disasters Emergency Committee
**www.dec.org.uk**

This is an umbrella organisation which launches and coordinates UK national appeals in response to major overseas disasters. The website has links to member organisations as well as information about appeals

## Global Issues
**www.globalissues.org**

A site which looks at various interrelated global issues that affect us all, including human rights, media, politics, trade, poverty and the environment, the arms trade, debt, children and conflict

## Peacenet
**www.igc.org**

An informative and easy-to-use website covering a wide range of topics such as human rights, the environment and social and economic justice

## 2 Rights and responsibilities

**Human Rights NOW!**
**www.hrnow.org**
A website full of useful information on human rights and links to major human-rights organisations

**BBC Children's Rights**
**www.bbc.co.uk/education/rights**
Information about children's rights, the effects of war on children, plus interviews with children around the world telling their own experiences. A user-friendly site

**Children of conflict**
**www.bbc.co.uk/worldservice/childrenofconflict**
To mark the 10th anniversary of the UN Convention on the Rights of the Child, the BBC's World Service tells the stories of children world-wide whose lives are blighted by war and poverty

**'I have a right to …'(BBC)**
**www.bbc.co.uk/worldservice/ihavearightto**
A BBC World Service website consisting of radio programmes in 13 languages; includes awareness-raising debates and events in participating countries

**UN Special Commission (UNSCOM)**
**www.un.org/depts/unscom**
Official reports from the UN Weapons inspection in Iraq detailing the main events in the Middle East from the end of the Gulf War in 1991 to Operation Desert Fox and beyond

**Permanent Mission of Iraq to the UN**
**www.iraqi-mission.org**
Pages from Iraq's representation at the UN featuring a profile of the country and the leader Saddam Hussein, the text of his speeches and detail of attempts to get sanctions imposed after the end of the Gulf War

## 3 Diversity

**Office for National Statistics**
**www.statistics.gov.uk**
A government website with a range of national statistics, including economic and social figures broken down into themed areas of the population and country; census data is also listed

**Britkid**
**www.britkid.org**
A website for young people about race, racism and growing up in Britain. In this interactive site you meet a group of nine young British people from different backgrounds. There are quizzes, quotes, lyrics and famous people from television, sport and music

**Artists Against Racism**
**www.vrx.net**
The website covers general issues on race and has quotes of support from a number of famous celebrities. It has a large database and research facility

**Commission for Racial Equality (CRE)**
**www.cre.gov.uk**
CRE is a government body for monitoring and advising on race issues in Britain. Useful and informative website

**Fight Racism**
**www.eumc.at**
This organisation's aim is to promote the work of the EU in the field of anti-racism through raising awareness of the migrant population's contributions to European society

## 4 Government services

**Ministry of Defence (MOD)**
**www.mod.uk**
The MOD web site includes information about the role of the MOD, a mission statement and information about defence policies

**Jane's**
**www.janes.com**
The ultimate source for defence, aerospace and transportation information. The website includes articles from current 'global flash points'

**NATO**
**www.nato.int**
A comprehensive site about NATO which includes policies and explanations of its role in various conflicts, eg in the former Yugoslavia

**Council for a Liveable World**
**www.clw.org**
An organisation committed to ridding the world of weapons of mass destruction and eliminating wasteful military spending. The site includes information on arms-control treaties. Much of the information is based on the USA but the website also covers the UN and arms as well as reports from other countries

**Greenpeace Nuclear Campaign Website**
**www.greenpeace.org**
Click from the homepage onto the 'nuclear' section for an informative site on nuclear power including information on testing weapons, waste and information on alternatives to nuclear power

## 5 Democracy

**International Monetary Fund (IMF)**
**www.imf.org**
Information about the IMF, including their 'mission', what the IMF does and how. The website also includes individual country profiles

**World Trade Organisation (WTO)**
**www.wto.org**
Explains clearly what the WTO is and how it works – a useful and informative reference site

**Trade and Development Centre**
**www.itd.org**
A website developed by both the World Bank and the WTO. It includes information on developing countries and the role of both organisations in trying to assist economic and social development. The section on 'frequently asked questions' gives an excellent insight into the work of these two international organisations

**Shell Group of Companies**
**www.shell.com**
A large and well-designed site from the oil giant. Includes a section on 'sensitive subjects': human rights, environmental issues and Shell in Nigeria

**Nestle**
**www.nestle.com**
Informative website, with a history of the company, press releases, policy on their global commitment and responsibilities. A good insight into one of the world's largest multinationals

## 6 Voluntary groups

**Disasters Emergency Committee**
**www.dec.org.uk**
This is an umbrella organisation which includes Action Aid, British Red Cross, CAFOD, CARE International, Christian Aid, Children's Aid Direct, Christian Children's Fund of Britain, Age Concern, Help the Aged, Merlin, Oxfam, Save The Children, Tearfund and World Vision UK

**Water Aid**
**www.wateraid.org**
A UK-based charity which helps the poorest communities in Africa and Asia by providing safe water supply and adequate sanitation. The site has a very good educational game

**International Committee of the Red Cross (ICRC)**
**www.icrc.org**
A large, well-designed site about the Red Cross including its history, country profiles and reports on the work it undertakes. There is a section on people and war and a project about the rules of modern warfare that aims to improve the humanitarian situation in conflicts around the world

## 8 Media

**BBC World Service Trust**
**www.bbc.co.uk/worldservicetrust**
The site uses the media to promote learning and development. It includes information from many different parts of the world

**Reuters Foundation**
**www.foundation.reuters.com**
An educational and humanitarian trust financed by Reuters, the global news, information and technology organisation. An easy-to-use site which includes information about Reuters and picture exhibitions

**Media Channel**
**www.oneworld.org/news**
A Oneworld project, with a website dedicated to global media issues

**Index on Censorship**
**www.indexoncensorship.org**
A magazine for free speech; the site includes interviews, reports and extracts on banned literature

**Camera**
**www.camera.org**
An interesting site which aims to promote a balanced coverage of the Middle East crisis. It includes a wide range of media sources from television news to newspapers

**UN Newscentre**
**www.un.org/newservice**
News articles from around the world and UN organisations

**Newspaper Education Trust**
**www.net.org**
This site encourages primary and secondary students to become interested in the world of newspapers. It provides information, support and training on setting up school newspapers as well as having a very useful resource bank

**War News**
**www.warnews.it**
The latest news and background information on all contemporary conflict around the world

## 7 Resolving conflict

**War News**
**www.warnews.it**
The latest news and background information on all contemporary conflict around the world

**War Child**
**www.warchild.org**
War Child is an independent organisation offering support to children affected by war. The site has information about the organisation's projects around the world, which are helping to rebuild young people's lives

**Child Soldiers**
**www.child-soldiers.org**
Information about the situation of child soldiers around the world and examples of things you can do to stop the recruitment of child soldiers

**Contemporary Conflicts in Africa**
**www.synapse.net**
An informative site, which has a wide range of resources on the prevention, management and resolution of violent conflicts in Africa

**The Institute of War and Peace Reporting**
**www.iwpr.net**
News and reports from Eastern Europe and the former Soviet Union

**Afronet**
**www.afronet.org.za**
This website about human rights and development in Africa has useful information on specific African countries

## 9 Global community

**Jubilee +**
**www.jubilee2000uk.org**
Information about the international movement and the 'Drop the Debt' campaign. The website has lots of ideas on how to lobby Western governments and banks to cancel the debts of third-world countries

**Grameen Bank**
**www.gdrc.org**
Information about the pioneering work of the Grameen bank; the site includes a section on statistical updates and a bibliography

**Survival International**
**www.survival.org**
This organisation is dedicated to supporting tribal people and their right to decide their own future. Information is given on how to become involved in campaigning as well as relevant news

**The Office for Social Justice - Debt Crisis**
**www.osjspm.org/debt**
Background information on the debt crisis and links to news, other organisations and campaigns. This also has some religious quotations relevant to the problem

**Concern**
**www.concern.ie**
An organisation that aims to help the world's poorest people to help themselves

# Glossary

**Adversary** – enemy or opponent

**Alleviate** – make something less severe or less painful

**Amnesty** – a general pardon, to forgive a person or group for political offences

**Aspire** – a strong desire to achieve something, something to work towards

**Boycott** – refuse to trade with someone or a country

**Civilians** – people not in the armed services or police

**Conflict** – a fight or struggle

**Consumption** – the quantity of products and natural resources being used up

**Controversial** – something about which people do not agree and discuss at length

**Convention** – an international agreement

**Corporation** – a business, company

**Covenant** – a legal document

**Demobilisation** – the end of armed force: sending all the soldiers back home and taking their weapons from them

**Deposes** – removes a person or group from power

**Developing countries** – countries that are poor and are trying to develop their economies

**Dictator** – a single person ruling a whole country, usually not elected

**Disarmament** – to reduce weapons and military forces

**Discriminate** – act unfairly against people on racial, religious, sexual grounds, etc

**Displaced** – forced a person to leave his/her own country because of war, fear, etc

**Diverse** – varied

**Endorsement** – backing or supporting someone or something

**Equitable** – fair and more equal

**Ethical** – morally correct

**Export** – goods sold abroad and leaving a country

**G8** – the group of the most powerful eight countries in the world

**Humanitarian relief** – support provided for people's basic needs

**Immigrants** – people who leave their country to come into yours

**Import** – goods bought abroad and coming into a country

**Independence** – the state a country is in when it rules itself

**Infrastructure** – the basic foundations of the country, including roads, bridges, sewers and communication systems

**Intermediary** – a go-between

**Intervene** – get involved in a conflict, between the two sides

**Kurds** – an ethnic-minority group in Iraq

**Liaison** – communication or cooperation

**Lobbying** – trying to get your point across to a decision-maker

**Migrant** – someone who leaves one country for another

**Military coup** – a violent or illegal seizure of power by the army

**Neutral** – not taking sides

**NHS** – National Health Service

**Reconciliation** – to settle an argument or disagreement

**Repression** – keep under control, often with force

**Resolution** – solving a problem

**Sanctions** – a punishment for breaking international law: for example, by restricting trade

**Solidarity** – unity, being together and supporting each other

**Tolerance** – allowing people to be different without interfering with them

**Treaties** – a formal agreement between two or more countries

**Truth and reconciliation commission** – a public hearing in which people involved in conflict come forward to admit what they did and ask for forgiveness

**UN Articles** – sections in a written document, which refer to specific rights

**Voluntary service** – giving your time for free

# Index